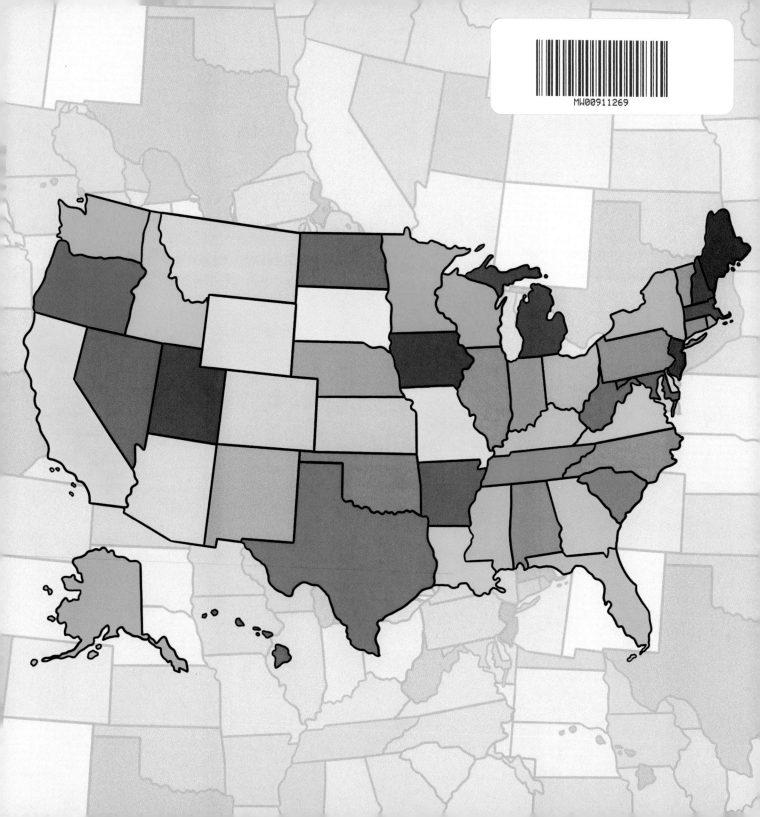

This book belongs to:

_____

LEARN the 50 States of America

with Bearific

KATELYN LONAS

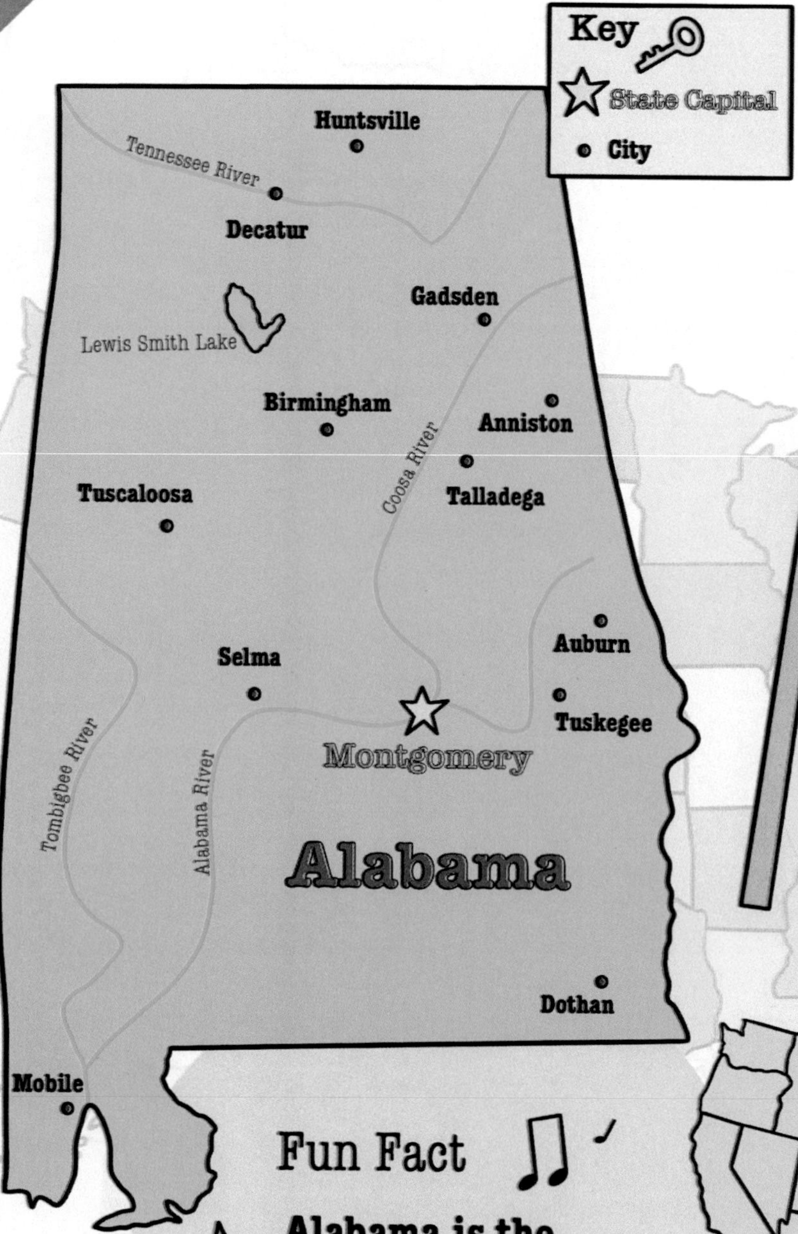

Key

State Capital

• City

Did you know?

Alabama became the 22nd state on December 14, 1819.

Huntsville

Tennessee River

Decatur

Lewis Smith Lake

Gadsden

Birmingham

Anniston

Coosa River

Tuscaloosa

Talladega

Selma

Auburn

Tuskegee

Montgomery

Alabama

Tombigbee River

Alabama River

Dothan

Mobile

Official State Flag

• is called the crimson cross of St. Andrew's
• was adopted in 1895
• was patterned from the Confederate Battle Flag

Fun Fact

Alabama is the official state song.

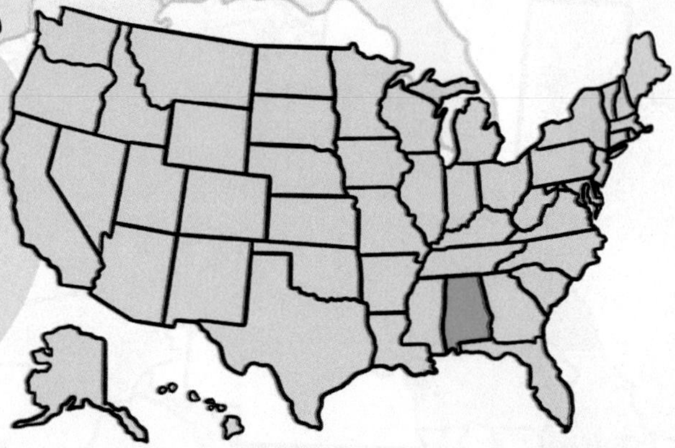

Official State Flower

- is the Camellia
- was designated as the state flower in 1959
- appears on the Alabama quarter

Alabama Quarter

- celebrates the spirit of courage
- features Helen Keller
- also has the state tree and flower

State Nicknames

- The Yellowhammer State
- The Cotton State
- The Heart of Dixie

Alabama is known for

- its iron and steel
- sweet tea
- football

Official State Bird

- is the Northern Flicker or Yellowhammer
- was designated as the state bird in 1927
- has been a symbol of Alabama since the Civil War

Official State Dessert

- is the Lane Cake
- was designated as the state dessert in 2016
- is a symbol of Southern culture

Alaska

Interesting Fact

The Alaska Highway was first built as a military supply road during World War II.

Did you know?

Alaska became the 49th state on January 3, 1959.

Barrow

Official State Flag

- was adopted in 1959
- stars represent the Big Dipper
- was designed by a 13 year old

Key

State Capital

City

Yukon River

Nome

Fairbanks

Kuskokwim River

Anchorage

Bethel

Valdez

Juneau

Sitka

Alaska

The Last Frontier

Aleutian Islands

N
W E
S

Fun Fact

The state motto is North to the Future.

Official State Fish

- is a King Salmon
- was designated as the state fish in 1962
- also called chinook salmon, spring salmon, quinnat, tyee, tule, and blackmouth salmon

Official State Flower

- is the alpine forget-me-not
- was adopted as the state flower in 1917
- grows well in Alaska in rocky or high mountain places

Alaska Quarter

- has the caption The Great Land
- features a grizzly bear
- also has the state fish and north star

Dinosaur Fossils Found in Alaska

- Albertosaurus
- Ankylosaur
- Edmontosaurus
- Pachycephalosaurus
- Pachyrhinosaurus
- Saurornitholestes
- Thescelosaurus
- Troödon

Official State Sport

- is dog mushing
- was designated as the state sport in 1972
- was a main form of transportation in many areas of Alaska

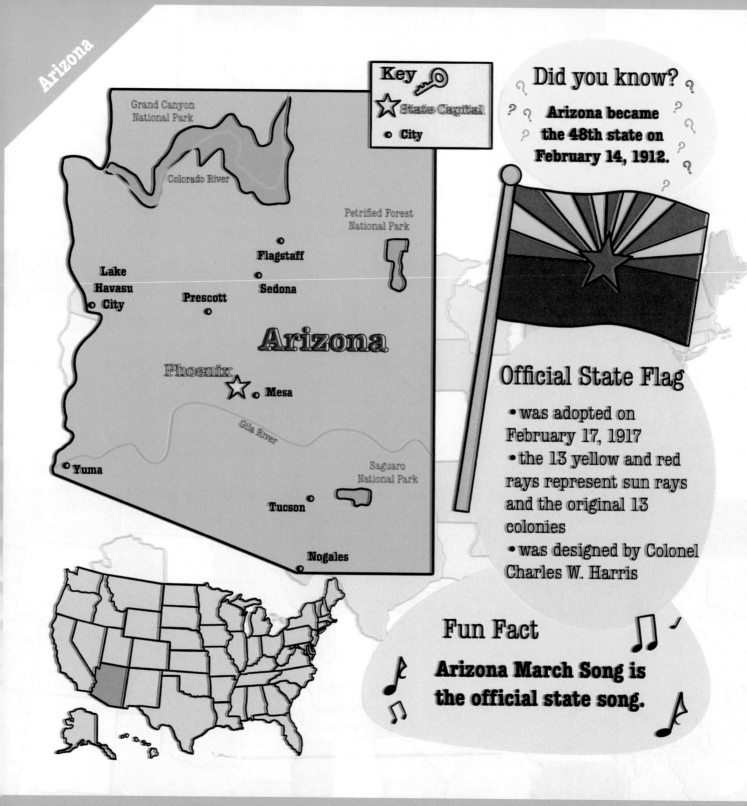

Arizona

Grand Canyon National Park

Colorado River

Key 🔑
⭐ State Capital
● City

Petrified Forest National Park

● Flagstaff

Lake Havasu City ●
● Prescott
● Sedona

Arizona

Phoenix ⭐ ● Mesa

Gila River

● Yuma

Saguaro National Park

Tucson ●

Nogales ●

Did you know?
Arizona became the 48th state on February 14, 1912.

Official State Flag
• was adopted on February 17, 1917
• the 13 yellow and red rays represent sun rays and the original 13 colonies
• was designed by Colonel Charles W. Harris

Fun Fact
Arizona March Song is the official state song.

Official State Amphibian

- is the Arizona tree frog called Hyla eximia
- was designated as the state amphibian in 1986
- is found in the mountains of central Arizona

Official State Flower

- is a Saguaro Cactus Blossom
- was designated as the state flower in 1931
- lives to an age of 150 to 200 years

Arizona Quarter

- says the state nickname The Grand Canyon
- features the Grand Canyon
- also has the Saguaro and other cacti

Official State Bird

- is the cactus wren
- was designated as the state bird in 1931
- they nest in cactus plants

Official State Butterfly

- is the two-tailed swallowtail butterfly
- was designated as the state butterfly in 2001
- is also called two-tailed tiger swallowtail

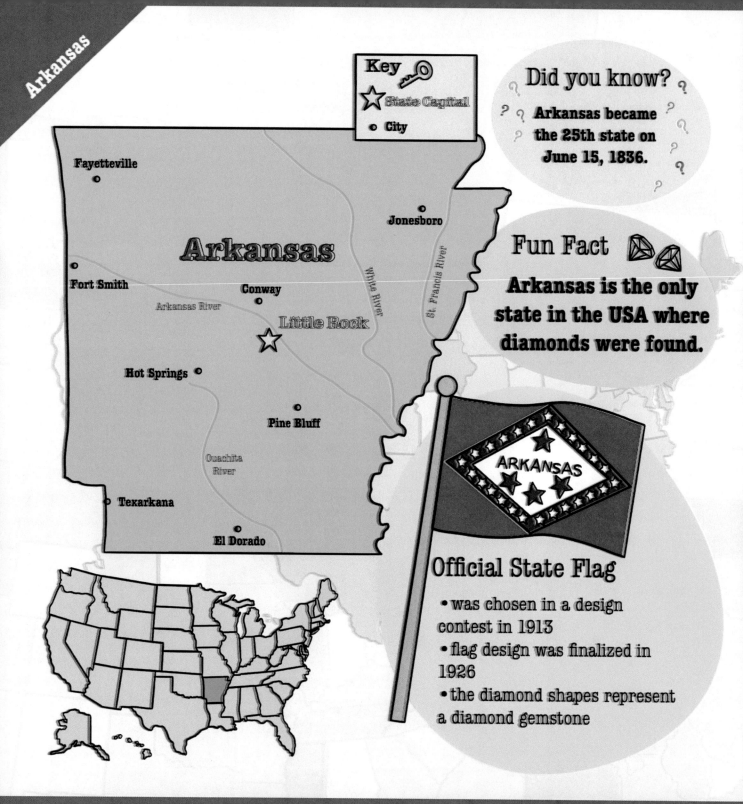

Key
★ State Capital
• City

Arkansas

Fayetteville

Jonesboro

Fort Smith

Conway

Arkansas River

White River

St. Francis River

Little Rock

Hot Springs

Pine Bluff

Ouachita River

Texarkana

El Dorado

Did you know?

Arkansas became the 25th state on June 15, 1836.

Fun Fact

Arkansas is the only state in the USA where diamonds were found.

ARKANSAS

Official State Flag

- was chosen in a design contest in 1913
- flag design was finalized in 1926
- the diamond shapes represent a diamond gemstone

Official State Insect

- is a honeybee
- was designated as the state insect in 1973
- lives in hives of up to 80,000 individuals

Official State Mammal

- is a white-tailed deer
- was designated as the state mammal in 1993
- are able to run up to 40 mph

Official State Beverage

- is milk
- was recognized as the state beverage in 1985
- dairy farming is important in Arkansas agriculture

Arkansas Quarter

- features a diamond
- features a mallard duck flying
- also has rice stalks and pine trees

Official State Musical Instrument

- is a fiddle
- was designated as the state musical instrument in 1985
- fiddles were an important part of life to the early pioneers

Official State Grape

- is the Cynthiana grape
- was designated as the state grape in 2009
- Arkansas has a rich heritage of vineyards

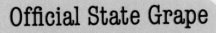

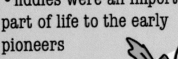

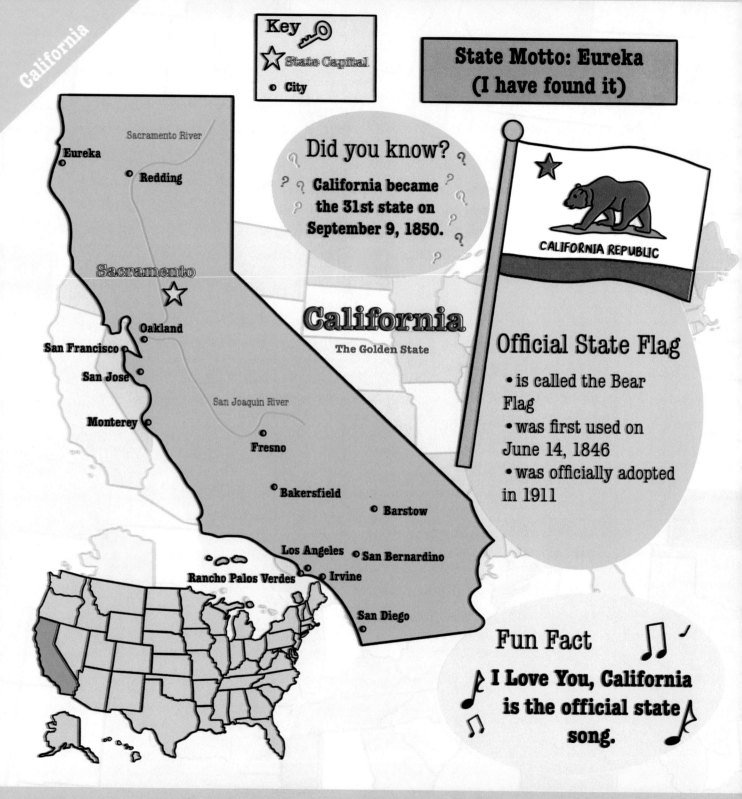

California

Key
★ State Capital
• City

State Motto: Eureka (I have found it)

Sacramento River

Eureka
Redding

Sacramento ★

Oakland
San Francisco
San Jose

Monterey

San Joaquin River

Fresno

Bakersfield

Barstow

Los Angeles • San Bernardino
Rancho Palos Verdes • Irvine

San Diego

Did you know?
California became the 31st state on September 9, 1850.

California
The Golden State

CALIFORNIA REPUBLIC

Official State Flag
• is called the Bear Flag
• was first used on June 14, 1846
• was officially adopted in 1911

Fun Fact ♫
I Love You, California is the official state song.

Official State Bird

- is the California quail
- was designated as the state bird in 1931
- known for their hardiness and adaptability

Official State Flower

- is the California poppy
- was designated as the state flower in 1903
- also known as the flame flower, la amapola, and copa de oro

Official State Fabric

- is denim
- was designated denim as the state fabric in 2016
- used to make many of things

California Quarter

- features John Muir an early advocate for wilderness conservation
- also features Yosemite National Park
- has the California condor

Official State Gold Rush Ghost Town

- is called Bodie
- was designated as the state gold rush ghost town in 2002
- became a town in 1877 and by 1879 had a population of 10,000 and 2,000 buildings

State Motto: Nil sine Numine (Nothing Without Providence)

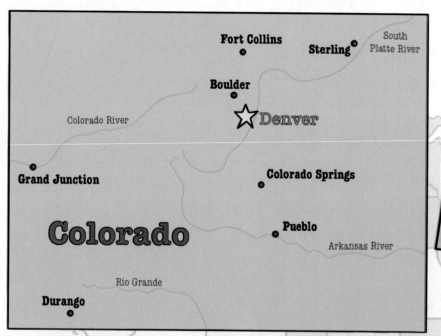

Fort Collins
Sterling
South Platte River
Boulder
Colorado River
⭐ Denver
Grand Junction
Colorado Springs
Colorado
Pueblo
Arkansas River
Rio Grande
Durango

Official State Flag

- was adopted on June 5, 1911
- the white symbolizes Colorado's snowcapped mountains
- the blue symbolizes clear blue skies

Key 🔑
⭐ State Capital
• City

Did you know?

Colorado became the 38th state on August 1, 1876.

Fun Fact 🎵

Where the Columbines Grow is the official state song.

Official State Flower

- is the white and lavender Rocky Mountain Columbine
- was designated as the state flower in 1899
- was discovered in 1820 on Pike's Peak by a mountain climber

Colorado Quarter

- features the Rocky mountains
- has one of the state's nicknames Colorful Colorado
- includes pine trees

Official State Fish

- is the greenback cutthroat trout
- was designated as the state fish in 1994
- was on the verge of extinction

Official State Bird

- is the lark bunting
- was designated as the state bird in 1931
- is a common sparrow of the Great Plains

Official State Insect

- is the Colorado hairstreak butterfly
- was designated as the state insect in 1996
- primary diet consists of tree sap, raindrops, and aphid honeydew

State Motto: Qui transtulit sustinet (He Who Transplanted Still Sustains)

Connecticut

Canaan

Stafford Springs

Putnam

☆ Hartford

Waterbury

Connecticut River

Danbury

Shelton

New London

Mystic

New Haven

Bridgeport

Norwalk

Stamford

Fun Fact

Yankee Doodle is the official state song.

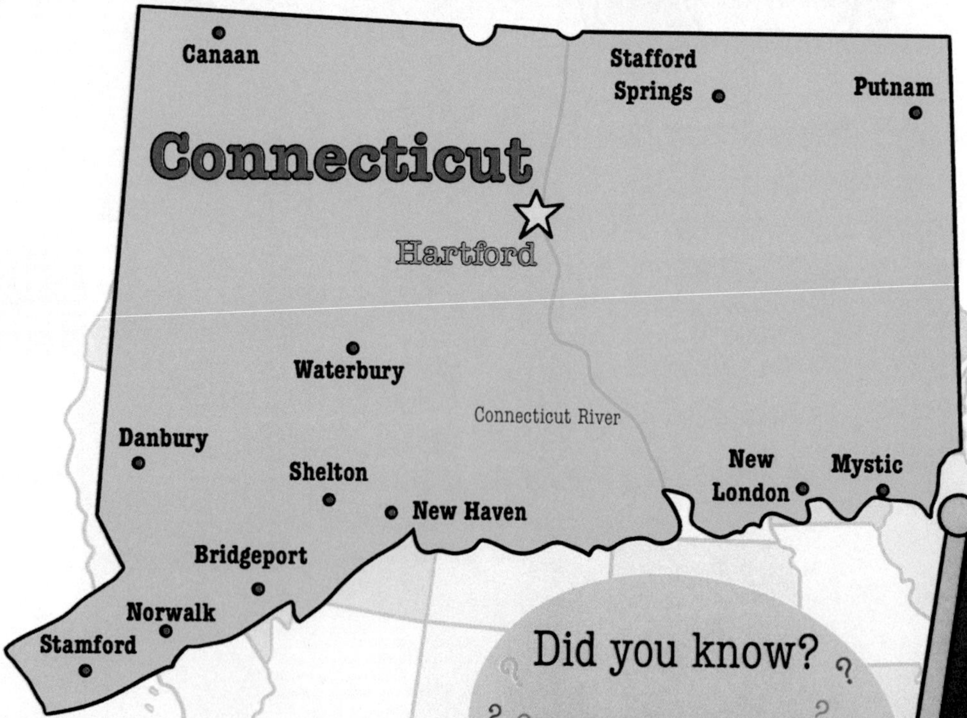

Key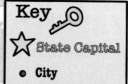

☆ State Capital

• City

Did you know?

Connecticut became the 5th state on January 9, 1788.

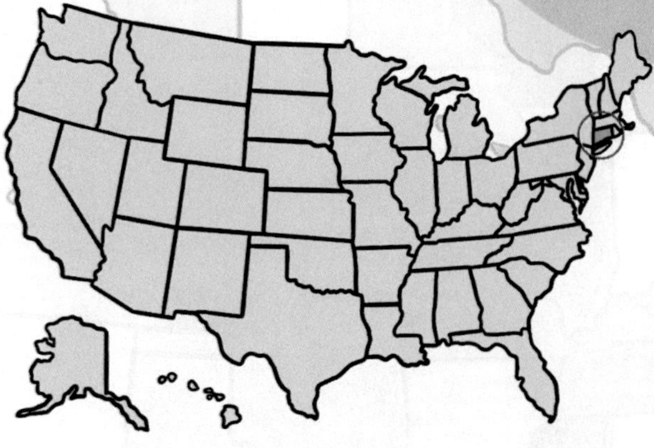

Official State Flag

• was adopted in 1897
• features 3 grapevines
• features a gold and silver rimmed shield

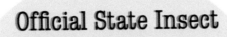

Official State Insect

- is the European praying mantis
- was designated as the state insect in 1977
- is a beneficial insect for farmers

Official State Bird

- is the American Robin
- was designated as the state bird in 1943
- one of America's favorite songbirds

Connecticut Quarter

- is the American Robin
- was designated as the state bird in 1943
- one of America's favorite songbirds

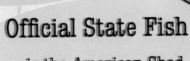

Official State Fish

- is the American Shad
- was designated as the state fish in 2003
- is important to history and the economy

Official State Flower

- is a mountain laurel
- was designated as the state flower in 1907
- is also called ivybush, calico bush, sheep laurel, lambkill, clamoun, and spoonwood

State Motto: Liberty and Independence

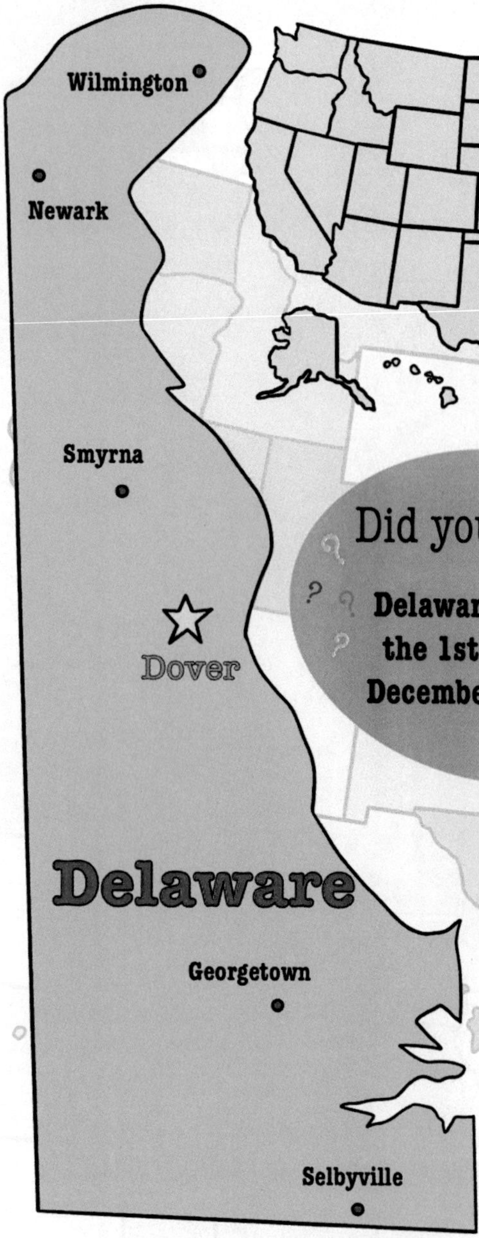

♪ Fun Fact ♪

Our Delaware is the official state song.

Wilmington

Newark

Smyrna

☆ Dover

Key 🔑
☆ State Capital
• City

Did you know?

Delaware became the 1st state on December 7, 1787.

Delaware

Georgetown

Selbyville

DECEMBER 7, 1787

Official State Flag

• was adopted on July 4, 1913
• features a soldier and a farmer
• has a white ribbon that says liberty and independence

Official State Fruit

- is strawberry
- was designated as the state fruit in 2010
- are an important part of Delaware's agricultural industry

Official State Bug

- is ladybug
- was adopted as the state bug in April 25, 1974
- also called lady beetle, ladybird beetle, or ladyfly,

Delaware Quarter

- features Caesar Rodney
- designated The First State as the state nickname on May 23, 2002
- was the first of the 13 original states to ratify the United States Constitution on December 7, 1787

Official State Fish

- is the weakfish
- was designated as the state fish in 1981
- also known as spotted sea trout, gray trout, yellow mouth, yellow fin trout, squeteague and tiderunner

Official State Sport

- is bicycling
- was designated as the state sport in 2014
- was ranked the 5th most bicycle friendly state in the United States in 2013

Florida

The Sunshine State

Pensacola

Tallahassee

Jacksonville

St. Augustine

Gainesville

Lake George

Daytona Beach

Orlando

Tampa

St. Petersburg

Lake Okeechobee

Fort Myers

Fort Lauderdale

Naples

Miami

Key West

Did you know?

Florida became the 27th state on March 3, 1845.

Key

⭐ State Capital

● City

Official State Flag

- was adopted in 1900
- has a red cross of St. Andrew on a white field
- in the center is the state seal

Fun Fact

Swanee River is the official state song.

Florida

Official State Honey

- is tupelo honey
- was designated as the state honey on March 16, 2016
- has been called one of the sweetest honeys on Earth

Florida Quarter

- features sabal palms the state tree
- has the saying Gateway to Discovery
- has a Spanish galleon and a space shuttle

Official State Pie

- is key lime pie
- was designated as the state pie in 2006
- is a dessert made from the juice of Key limes

Official State Saltwater Mammal

- is a dolphin
- was designated as the state saltwater mammal in 1975
- are considered to be among the most intelligent of animals

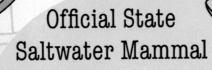

Official State Fruit

- is orange
- was designated as the state fruit in 2005
- are a major part of Florida's economy

Official State Beverage

- is orange juice
- was designated as the state beverage in 1967
- production of orange juice is a multi-million dollar industry

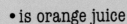

Georgia

Dalton

Rome

Chattahoochee River

Athens

☆ Atlanta

Augusta

Georgia

Peach State

Macon

Columbus

Savannah

Key ⚷
☆ State Capital
● City

Americus

Valdosta

Did you know?
Georgia became the
4th state on
January 2, 1788.

Official State Flag
• was designed in May,
2003
• has three pillars
symbolizing the three
branches of government
in the USA
• the banner says
constitution, justice,
wisdom, and moderation

Fun Fact ♫ ♪
Georgia on My Mind is
the official state song.

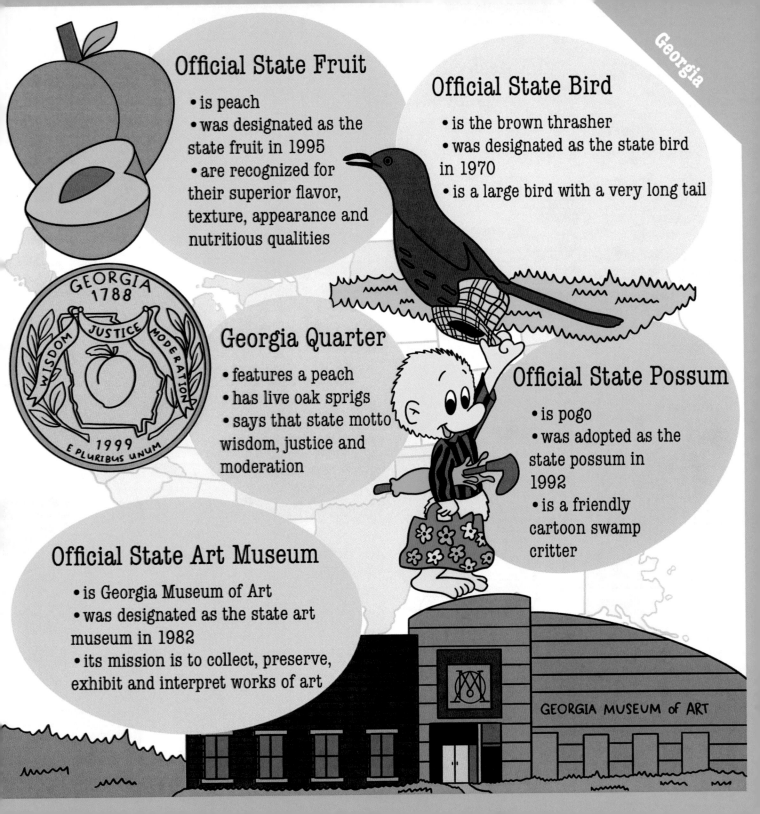

Official State Fruit

- is peach
- was designated as the state fruit in 1995
- are recognized for their superior flavor, texture, appearance and nutritious qualities

Official State Bird

- is the brown thrasher
- was designated as the state bird in 1970
- is a large bird with a very long tail

Georgia Quarter

- features a peach
- has live oak sprigs
- says that state motto wisdom, justice and moderation

Official State Possum

- is pogo
- was adopted as the state possum in 1992
- is a friendly cartoon swamp critter

Official State Art Museum

- is Georgia Museum of Art
- was designated as the state art museum in 1982
- its mission is to collect, preserve, exhibit and interpret works of art

Interesting Fact

Hawaii is the only state that grows coffee.

Kapaa

Kauai

Niihau

Oahu

Kaneohe

Waipahu

Honolulu

Did you know?

Hawaii became the 50th state on August 21, 1959.

Fun Fact

Hawaii Ponoi is the official state song.

Molokai

Kaunakaki

Hawaii

Aloha State

Kahului   **Maui**

Lanai

Kahoolawe

Key
⭐ State Capital
● City

Kailua

Hilo

Captain Cook

Hawaii

Official State Flag

• was commissioned by King Kamehameha I of Hawaii in 1816
• eight stripes of white, red and blue represent the eight main islands of Hawaii
• the upper left corner honors Hawaii's long relationship with the British

Official State Flower

- is yellow hibiscus
- was designated as the state flower in 1988
- is found only in Hawaii

Hawaii Quarter

- features a statue of Kamehameha I
- has the state motto Ua Mau ke Ea o ka 'Āina i ka Pono meaning the life of the land is perpetuated in righteousness
- has the outline of Hawaii

HAWAII 1959

UA MAU KE EA O KA 'ĀINA I KA PONO

2008

E PLURIBUS UNUM

Official State Modern Musical Instrument

- is the ukulele
- was designated as the state modern musical instrument in 2015
- commonly played during a traditional hula dance

Official State Insect

- is the pulelehua
- was designated as the state insect in 2009
- also known as the kamehameha butterfly

Official State Bird

- is the nene
- was designated as the state bird in 1957
- also known as the Hawaiian goose

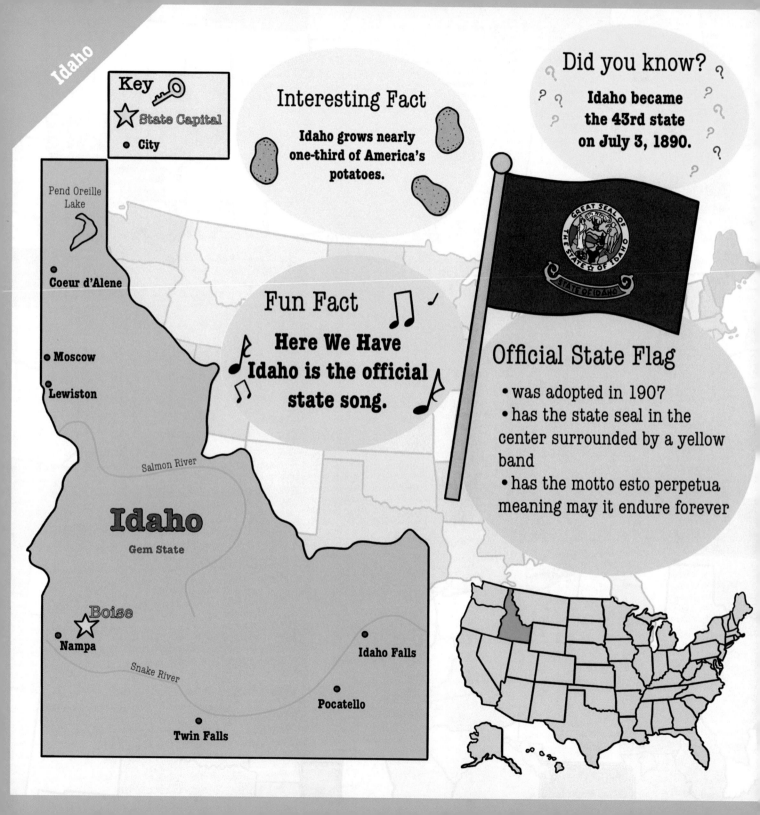

Idaho

Key
☆ State Capital
• City

Interesting Fact

Idaho grows nearly one-third of America's potatoes.

Did you know?

Idaho became the 43rd state on July 3, 1890.

Fun Fact

Here We Have Idaho is the official state song.

Official State Flag

- was adopted in 1907
- has the state seal in the center surrounded by a yellow band
- has the motto esto perpetua meaning may it endure forever

Pend Oreille Lake

Coeur d'Alene

Moscow

Lewiston

Salmon River

Idaho
Gem State

Boise

Nampa

Snake River

Idaho Falls

Pocatello

Twin Falls

Official State Bird

- is the mountain bluebird
- was designated as the state bird in 1931
- prefers to stay in more open habitats

Official State Flower

- is the Syringa
- was designated as the state flower in 1931
- sometimes called mock orange

IDAHO
1890
ESTO PERPETUA
2007
E PLURIBUS UNUM

Idaho Quarter

- features a peregrine falcon
- has a map of Idaho with a star
- says the state motto

Official State Fruit

- is huckleberry
- was designated as the state fruit in 2000
- grows at elevations between 2,000 and 11,000 feet

Official State Raptor

- is the peregrine falcon
- was designated as the state raptor in 2004
- has been called the fastest animal on the planet in its hunting dive

Rockford

Chicago

DeKalb

Rock Island

Peoria

Bloomington

Quincy

☆ Springfield

Illinois

Prairie State

Alton

Rend Lake

Carbondale

Key
☆ State Capital
• City

ILLINOIS

Official State Flag

• was redesigned in 1970
• has the Illinois state seal is in the center
• has the dates 1818 which refers to the year Illinois became a state and 1868 which refers to the date the state seal was redesigned

Fun Fact
Illinois is the
official state song.

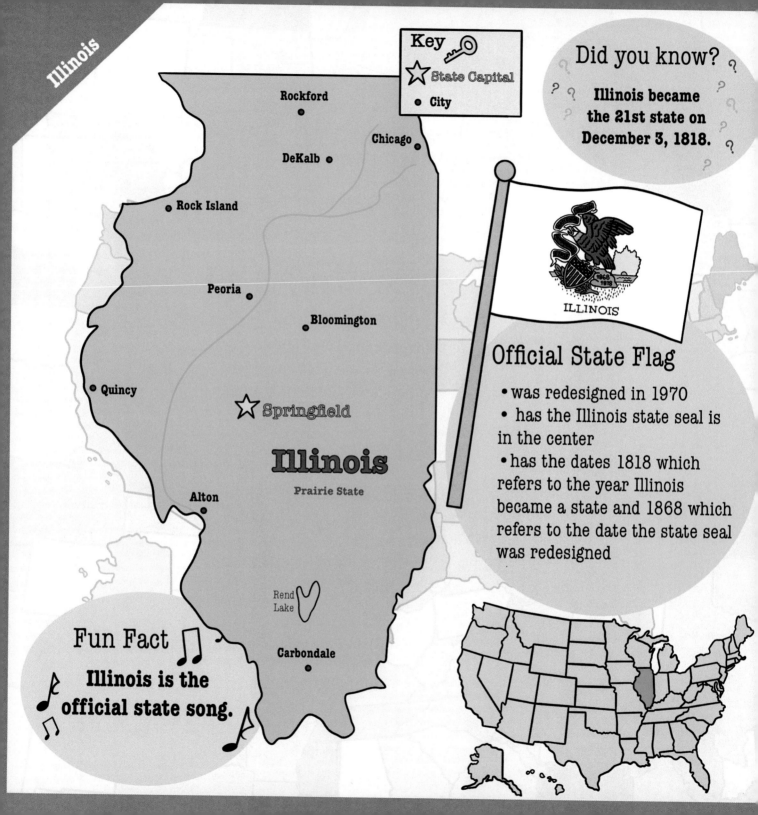

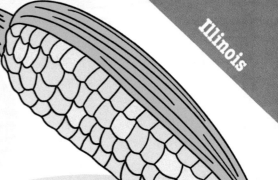

Official State Snack Food

- is popcorn
- was designated as the state snack food in 2003
- has 333 farms in Illinois that grow popcorn on 47,000 acres

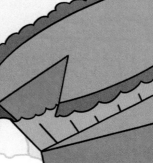

Illinois Quarter

- features young Abraham Lincoln
- has the state slogan Land of Lincoln
- has a farm scene, the Chicago skyline and 21 stars

Official State Vegetable

- is corn
- was designated as the state vegetable in 2015
- is also the state grain

Official State Pie

- is pumpkin pie
- was designated as the state pie in 2015
- 85% of consumed pumpkin in the U.S. comes from Illinois

Official State Fish

- is the Bluegill
- was designated as the state fish in 1986
- are most abundant in clear lakes

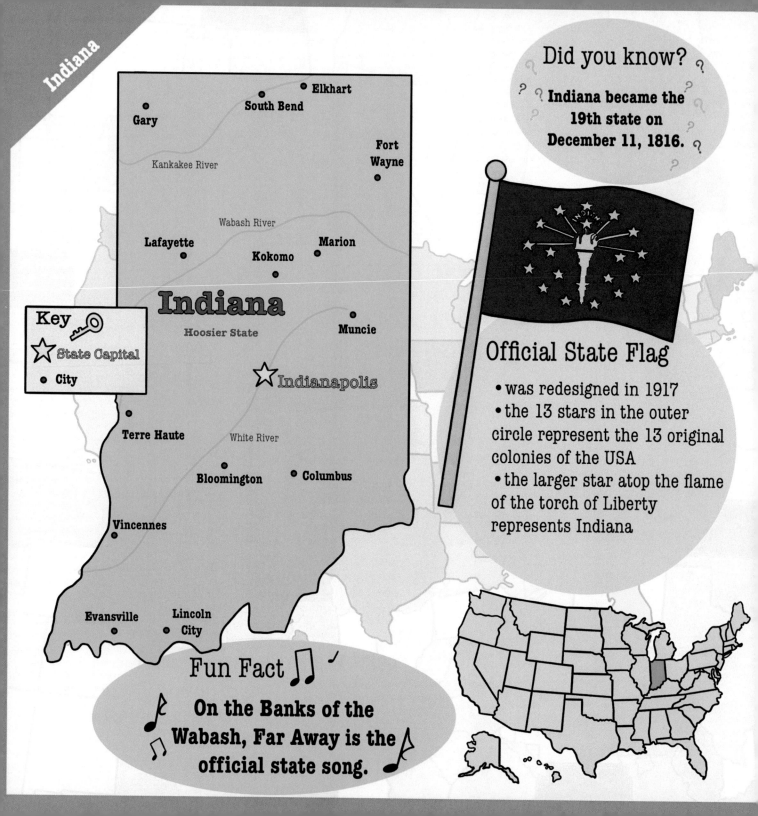

Indiana

Elkhart
South Bend
Gary
Fort Wayne
Kankakee River
Wabash River
Lafayette
Marion
Kokomo

Indiana

Hoosier State

Muncie

☆ Indianapolis

Key 🔑
☆ State Capital
• City

Terre Haute
White River

Bloomington
Columbus

Vincennes

Evansville
Lincoln City

Did you know?

Indiana became the 19th state on December 11, 1816.

Official State Flag

• was redesigned in 1917
• the 13 stars in the outer circle represent the 13 original colonies of the USA
• the larger star atop the flame of the torch of Liberty represents Indiana

Fun Fact ♫

On the Banks of the Wabash, Far Away is the official state song.

Official State Flower

- is a peony
- was designated as the state flower in 1957
- are also extensively grown as ornamental plants

Indiana Quarter

- features the state motto crossroads of America
- has an IndyCar
- has the outline of Indiana with 19 stars

Official State Bird

- is the northern cardinal
- was designated as the state bird in 1933
- one of America's favorite backyard birds

Official State Seal

- has a woodsman chopping a tree
- has the date Indiana entered the union 1816
- has a buffalo jumping over a log and sycamore trees

Official State Tree

- is the tulip poplar
- was designated as the state tree in 1931
- also called yellow poplar, tulip tree and canoe tree

State Motto: Our liberties we prize and our rights we will maintain

Map of Iowa

- Mason City
- Cedar River
- Iowa River
- Sioux City
- Waterloo
- Dubuque
- **Iowa**
- Ames
- Cedar Rapids
- Des Moines River
- Davenport
- ★ Des Moines
- Iowa City
- Council Bluffs
- Ottumwa
- Burlington

Fun Fact

The Song of Iowa is the official state song.

Key

★ State Capital

• City

Did you know?

Iowa became the 29th state on December 28, 1846.

Major Lake: Lake Red Rock

Official State Flag

IOWA

- was adopted in 1921
- symbolizes that Iowa became a part of the US as part of the Louisiana Purchase
- on the ribbon it says our liberties we prize and our rights we will maintain

Interesting Fact

Strawberry Point is the home of the world's largest strawberry.

Official State Flower

- is the wild prairie rose
- was adopted as the state flower in 1897
- has been around for about 35 million years

Iowa Quarter

- features Grant Wood's Arbor Day painting
- is a painting of a one-room schoolhouse with teacher and students planting a tree
- has the caption Foundation in Education

IOWA
1846
FOUNDATION
IN EDUCATION
GRANT WOOD
2004
E PLURIBUS UNUM

Official State Bird

- is the eastern goldfinch
- was designated as the state bird in 1933
- also called American goldfinch or wild canary

THE GREAT SEAL OF THE STATE OF IOWA
WE PRIZE AND OUR RIGHTS
OUR LIBERTIES WE WILL MAINTAIN

Official State Seal

- was one of the initial acts of Iowa's first Legislature in 1847
- has a citizen soldier standing in a wheat field
- has the Mississippi River in the background

State Motto: Ad astra per aspera (to the stars through difficulties)

Fun Fact

Home on the Range is the official state song.

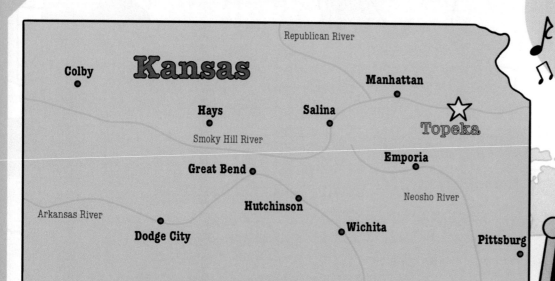

Kansas

Republican River

Colby

Hays

Salina

Manhattan

☆ Topeka

Smoky Hill River

Emporia

Great Bend

Neosho River

Hutchinson

Arkansas River

Wichita

Dodge City

Pittsburg

Key

☆ State Capital

● City

Major Lakes:
Tuttle Creek Reservoir,
Cheney Reservoir,
Waconda Lake

Did you know?

Kansas became the 34th state on January 29, 1861.

KANSAS

Official State Flag

• was adopted in 1927
• has a sunflower and the state seal of Kansas
• has the state motto ad astra per aspera on the ribbon

Interesting Fact

It was once against the law to serve ice cream on cherry pie in Kansas.

Official State Flower

- is the wild native sunflower
- was designated as the state flower and floral emblem in 1903
- sunflower heads consist of 1,000 to 2,000 individual flowers joined together

Kansas Quarter

- features an American buffalo
- also features sunflowers
- has the year 1861 which is when Kansas became a state

KANSAS
1861
2005
E PLURIBUS UNUM

Official State Reptile

- is the ornate box turtle
- was designated as the state reptile in 1986
- can completely withdraw its legs, tail, head, and neck into a sturdy shell

Official State Bird

- is the western meadowlark
- was designated as the state bird in 1937
- estimated that at least 65-70% of their diet consists of beetles, cutworms, caterpillars, grasshoppers, spiders, sow bugs, and snails

Fun Fact
My Old Kentucky Home is the official state song.

State Motto: United we stand, divided we fall

Frankfort

Louisville ☆   Lexington

Kentucky

Owensboro

Somerset

Paducah

Bowling Green

Key
☆ State Capital
● City

Major Lakes:
Lake Cumberland, Kentucky Lake, Lake Barkley

Did you know?
Kentucky became the 15th state on June 1, 1792.

COMMONWEALTH OF KENTUCKY
UNITED WE STAND
DIVIDED WE FALL

Official State Flag

• was adopted in 1918
• says united we stand divided we fall
• has a pioneer and a statesman shaking hands with goldenrod flowers on the bottom

Interesting Fact
Cheeseburgers were first served in 1934 in Louisville.

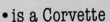

Official State Sports Car

- is a Corvette
- was designated as the state sports car in 2010
- the National Corvette Museum is located at Bowling Green, Kentucky

Official State Fruit

- is blackberry
- was designated as the state fruit in 2004
- also called bramble berry or bramble raspberry

Official State Wild Game Animal

- is the eastern gray squirrel
- was designated as the state wild animal game in 1968
- buries food in hundreds of different locations

Kentucky Quarter

- features a thoroughbred racehorse
- also features the historic Federal Hill mansion in Bardstown
- has the state song my old Kentucky home

Key
⭐ State Capital
● City

Interesting Fact

Louisiana has the tallest state capital building in the United States.

Did you know?

Louisiana became the 18th state on April 30, 1812.

Shreveport

Monroe

Ruston

Red River

Ouachita River

Nachitoches

Alexandria

Louisiana

Pelican State

Baton Rouge ⭐

Lafayette

Lake Pontchartrain

Mississippi River

New Orleans

Morgan City

Houma

Official State Flag

• was adopted in 1912
• has a white pelican mother feeding her three chicks
• this pelican represents the state protecting the people and their land

UNION JUSTICE CONFIDENCE

Fun Fact

You Are My Sunshine is the official state song.

Official State Bird

- is the brown pelican
- was designated as the state bird in 1966
- appears on Louisiana's state flag, state seal, the state painting, and many other symbols and icons

Official State Vegetable Plant

- is the Creole tomato
- was designated as the state vegetable plant in 2003
- some calls it tomato, tomaahto, or Creoles

Louisiana Quarter

- features the state bird
- has a musical symbol for New Orleans Jazz
- has an outline of the original Louisiana purchase

Official State Symbol

- is the fleur-de-lis
- was designated as the state symbol in 2008
- fleur-de-lis is a stylized lily or iris

Official State Sport

- is the pirogue
- was designated as the state sport in 2012
- is particularly popular in the vast Cajun culture of south Louisiana

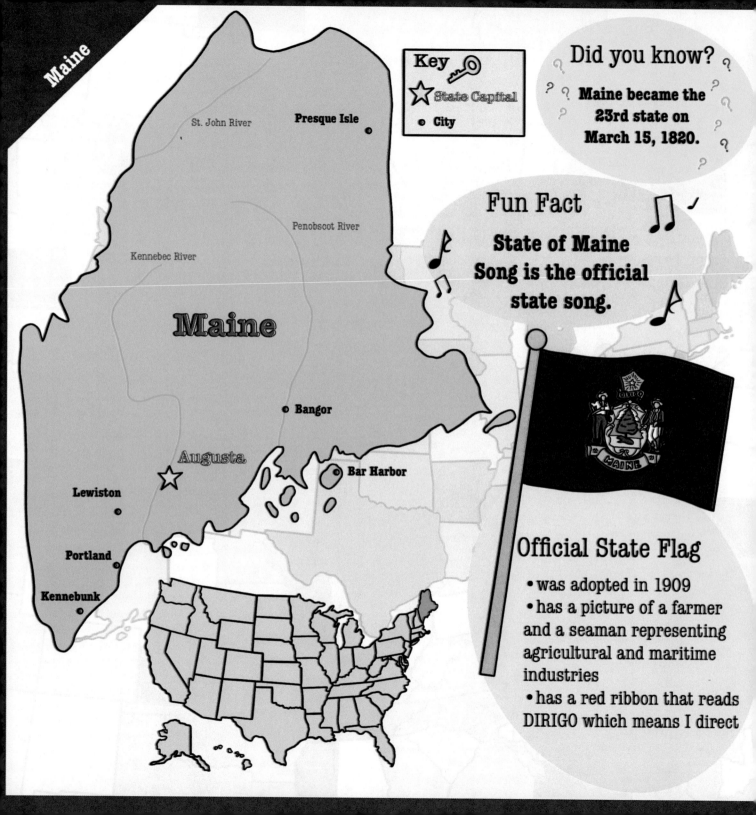

Maine

Key
⚷ State Capital
• City

Did you know?
Maine became the 23rd state on March 15, 1820.

Fun Fact
State of Maine Song is the official state song.

St. John River

Presque Isle

Penobscot River

Kennebec River

Maine

• Bangor

Augusta
☆

Lewiston
•

• Bar Harbor

Portland
•

Kennebunk
•

Official State Flag
• was adopted in 1909
• has a picture of a farmer and a seaman representing agricultural and maritime industries
• has a red ribbon that reads DIRIGO which means I direct

Official State Sweetener

- is pure Maine maple syrup
- was designated as the state sweetener in 2015
- the fourth Sunday every March is Maple Sunday in Maine

Official State Treat

- is whoopie pie
- was designated as the state treat in 2010
- has been baked in Maine since 1925

Maine Quarter

- features Pemaquid Point lighthouse
- also features a schooner at sea
- has the state tree called white pine

Official State Berry

- is wild blueberry
- was designated as the state berry in 1991
- is found in mostly rocky terrain

Official State Crustacean

- is lobster
- was designated as the state crustacean in 2016
- Maine is the state that produces the most lobster in the United States

State Motto: Fatti Maschii, Parole Femine (Manly Deeds, Womanly Words)

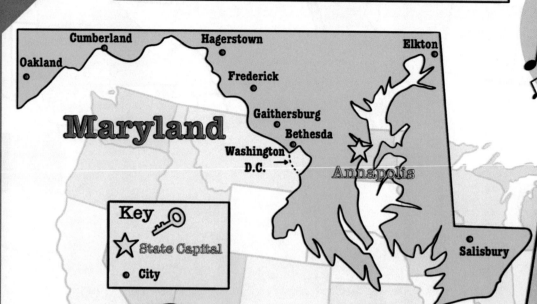

Fun Fact
Maryland, My Maryland is the official state song.

Major Lakes:
Lake Oakland,
Deep Creek Lake,
Prettyboy Reservoir,
Loch Raven Reservoir

Did you know?
Maryland became the 7th state on April 28, 1788.

Official State Flag
• was adopted in 1904
• the black and yellow part are from Lord Calvert's family
• the white and red part are either from the Mynnes, the Crosslands, Calvert's maternal family, or his wife's family

Interesting Fact
The first dental school in the United States opened in Maryland.

Official State Insect

- the Baltimore checkerspot butterfly
- was designated as the arthropodic emblem in 1973
- lives mostly in boggy habitats

Official State Dessert

- is the Smith Island cake
- was designated as the state dessert in 2008
- can be stacked up to 12 layers high

Maryland Quarter

- features the dome of the State House
- also features the state tree called white oak clusters
- has Maryland's nickname the old line state

Official State Bird

- is the Baltimore oriole
- was designated as the state bird in 1947
- males are a black golden color and females are a brown orange color

Massachusetts

**State Motto: Ense petit placidam sub libertate quietem
(By the sword we seek peace, but peace only under liberty)**

Key
🔑 State Capital
⭐ City

Lowell
Concord
Pittsfield
Amherst
Worcester
Boston
Springfield
Brockton
Cape Cod
Plymouth
New Bedford
Fall River

Major Lake:
Quabbin Reservoir

Massachusetts

Fun Fact
All Hail to Massachusetts is the official state song.

Did you know?
Massachusetts became the 6th state on February 6, 1788.

Official State Flag
• was adopted in 1971
• has Native American carrying a bow and arrow
• says the state motto ense petit placidam sub libertate quietem on the ribbon

Official State Flower

- is the mayflower
- was adopted as the state flower in 1918
- also known as ground laurel or trailing arbutus

Official State Cookie

- is chocolate chip cookie
- was adopted as the state cookie in 1997
- a third grade class proposed the bill for the chocolate chip cookie

Official State Reptile

- is the garter snake
- was adopted as the state reptile in 2007
- also called garden snake, gardener snake, and ribbon snake

Massachusetts Quarter

- features a minuteman
- has Massachusetts nickname The Bay State
- also has the the outline of Massachusetts

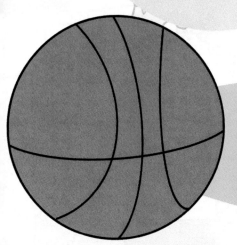

Official State Sport

- is basketball
- was adopted as the state sport in 2006
- the game of basketball was invented in 1891

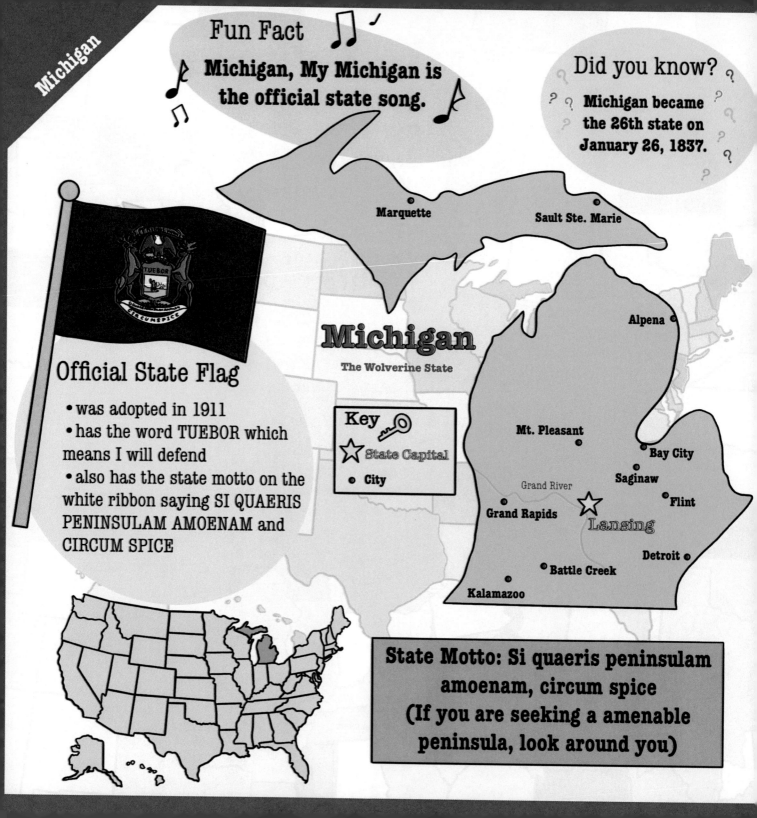

Michigan

Fun Fact
Michigan, My Michigan is the official state song.

Did you know?
Michigan became the 26th state on January 26, 1837.

Marquette

Sault Ste. Marie

Michigan
The Wolverine State

Alpena

Official State Flag

- was adopted in 1911
- has the word TUEBOR which means I will defend
- also has the state motto on the white ribbon saying SI QUAERIS PENINSULAM AMOENAM and CIRCUM SPICE

Key
State Capital
• **City**

Mt. Pleasant

Bay City

Saginaw

Grand River

Flint

Grand Rapids

Lansing

Detroit

Battle Creek

Kalamazoo

State Motto: Si quaeris peninsulam amoenam, circum spice
(If you are seeking a amenable peninsula, look around you)

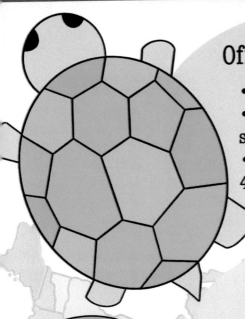

Official State Reptile

- is the painted turtle
- was designated as the state reptile in 1995
- can range in length from 4 to 10 inches

Official State Flower

- is apple blossom
- was designated as the state flower in 1897
- Michigan has been one of the leading producers of apples

Official State Bird

- is the robin redbreast
- was designated as the state bird in 1931
- were named by early settlers

Michigan Quarter

- features the state outline within the Great Lakes system
- also features the state nickname Great Lakes State
- has the year 1837 which is when Michigan became the 26th state

Official State Wildflower

- is the dwarf lake iris
- was designated as the state wildflower in 1998
- is found on the coastlines of northern Lake Michigan

Minnesota
North Star State

Did you know?
Minnesota became the 32nd state on May 11, 1858.

International Falls

Lake Itasca

Moorhead

Duluth

Mississippi River

St. Cloud

Minneapolis

Minnesota River

St. Paul

Mankato

Rochester

Key
⭐ State Capital
• City

Official State Flag
• was adopted in 1893
• has the state motto, L'ETOILE DU NORD which means the star of the north
• the pictures is a farmer plowing a field and an Indian riding a horse

Fun Fact
Hail Minnesota is the official state song.

Official State Muffin

- is blueberry muffin
- was designated as the state muffin in 1988
- the bill was requested by a third grade class

Official State Sport

- is ice hockey
- was designated as the state sport in 2009
- ice hockey was suggested by sixth graders to adopt it as the state sport

Minnesota Quarter

- features Minnesota's nickname Land of 10,000 Lakes
- also features the state bird called common loon
- has the state tree called red pine

Official State Bird

- is the common loon
- was designated as the state bird in 1961
- are known for their cries and echoing calls

Official State Mushroom

- is morel mushrooms
- was designated as the state mushroom in 1984
- is found mostly in southeastern Minnesota

Mississippi

Yazoo River

Corinth

Tupelo

Greenville

Yazoo City

Pearl River

Jackson

Meridian

Vicksburg

Natchez

Hattiesburg

Gulfport   Biloxi

Key
🔑
⭐ State Capital
• City

Did you know?

Mississippi became the 20th state on December 10, 1817.

IN GOD WE TRUST

Official State Flag

- says IN GOD WE TRUST
- has the state flower magnolia
- has a gold star which represents Native American tribes

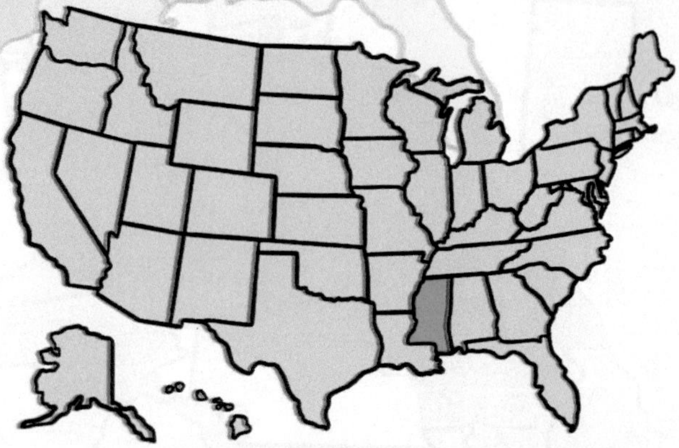

Fun Fact

Go Mis-sis-sip-pi is the official state song.

Official State Flower

- is magnolia
- was designated as the state flower in 1952
- was chosen by schoolchildren through an election in 1900

Official State Bird

- is the mockingbird
- was designated as the state bird in 1944
- can sing up to 200 songs

Mississippi Quarter

- features the state flower magnolias
- also features the state nickname The Magnolia State
- has the year 1817 which was when Mississippi became a state

MISSISSIPPI 1817
The Magnolia State
2002
E PLURIBUS UNUM

Official State Mammal

- is the red fox
- was designated as the state mammal in 1997
- plays an important role in rodent and insect control

Official State Fossil

- is the prehistoric whales
- was designated as the state fossil in 1981
- the prehistoric whales are Basilosaurus cetoides and Zygorhiza kochii

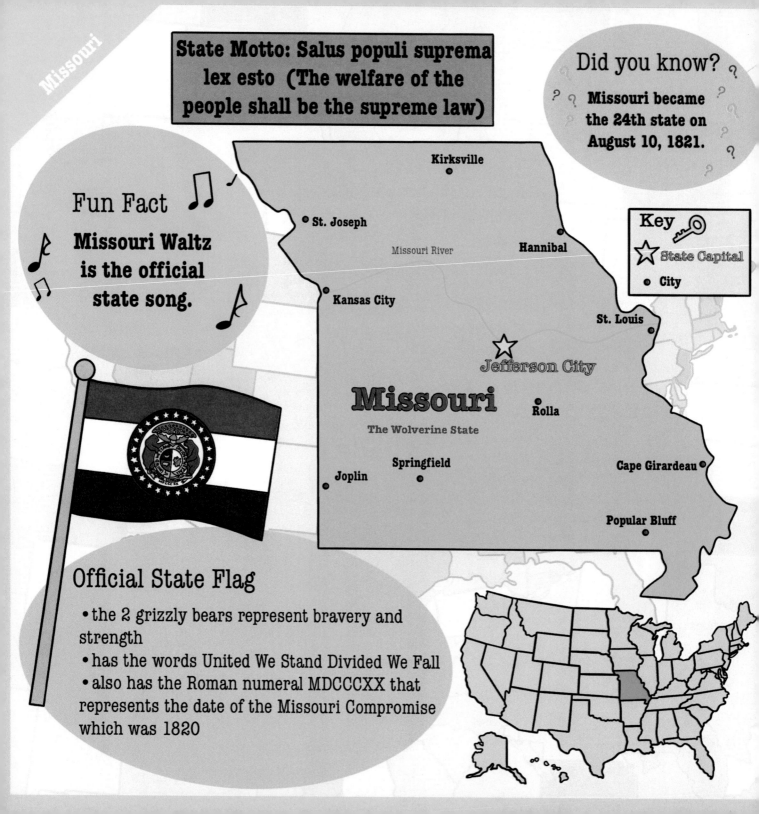

Missouri

State Motto: Salus populi suprema lex esto (The welfare of the people shall be the supreme law)

Did you know? Missouri became the 24th state on August 10, 1821.

Fun Fact
Missouri Waltz is the official state song.

Kirksville

St. Joseph

Missouri River

Hannibal

Key
State Capital
City

Kansas City

St. Louis

Jefferson City

Missouri
The Wolverine State

Rolla

Springfield

Cape Girardeau

Joplin

Popular Bluff

Official State Flag

• the 2 grizzly bears represent bravery and strength
• has the words United We Stand Divided We Fall
• also has the Roman numeral MDCCCXX that represents the date of the Missouri Compromise which was 1820

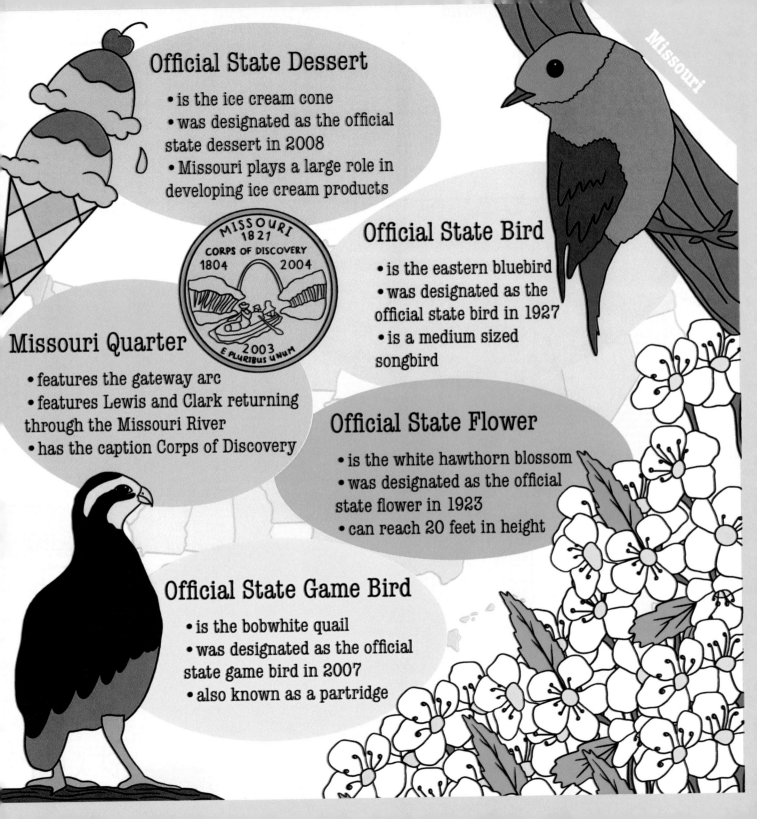

Missouri

Official State Dessert

- is the ice cream cone
- was designated as the official state dessert in 2008
- Missouri plays a large role in developing ice cream products

Official State Bird

- is the eastern bluebird
- was designated as the official state bird in 1927
- is a medium sized songbird

Missouri Quarter

- features the gateway arc
- features Lewis and Clark returning through the Missouri River
- has the caption Corps of Discovery

Official State Flower

- is the white hawthorn blossom
- was designated as the official state flower in 1923
- can reach 20 feet in height

Official State Game Bird

- is the bobwhite quail
- was designated as the official state game bird in 2007
- also known as a partridge

Key
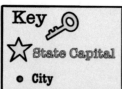
⭐ State Capital
• City

Interesting Fact
Montana's nickname is the Treasure State.

Did you know?
Montana became the 41st state on November 8, 1889.

Fun Fact
Montana is the official state song.

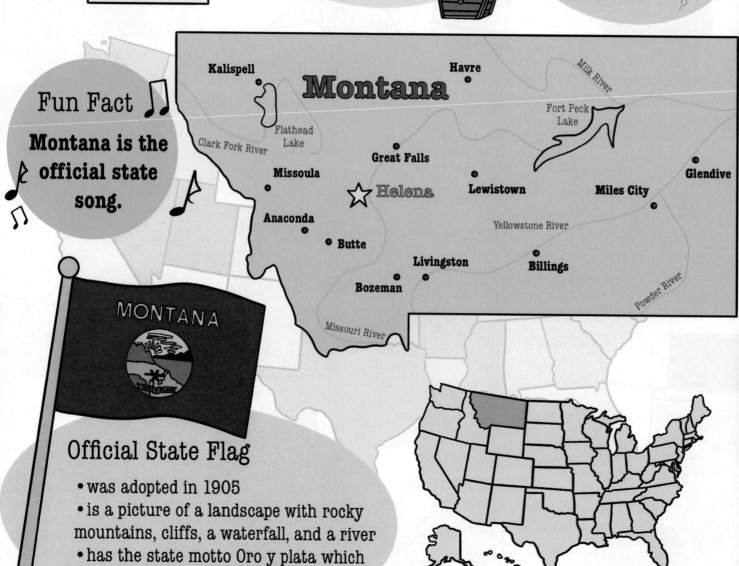

Montana

Kalispell
Havre
Milk River
Fort Peck Lake
Flathead Lake
Clark Fork River
Great Falls
Glendive
Missoula
⭐ Helena
Lewistown
Miles City
Anaconda
Yellowstone River
Butte
Livingston
Billings
Bozeman
Powder River
Missouri River

Official State Flag
• was adopted in 1905
• is a picture of a landscape with rocky mountains, cliffs, a waterfall, and a river
• has the state motto Oro y plata which means Gold and Silver

MONTANA

Official State Animal

- is the grizzly bear
- was designated as the state animal in 1983
- are the biggest carnivores in America

Official State Seal

- features the great waterfalls of the Missouri River
- has a pick, a shovel, and a plow which symbolizes Montana's mining and farming history
- has the words The Great Seal of the State of Montana and the state motto Oro y Plata

Official State Flower

- is the bitterroot
- was designated as the state flower in 1895
- Native Americans and Indians used the roots for food and trade

Montana Quarter

- features a bison skull
- also features the Missouri River
- has one of Montana's nicknames Big Sky Country

Official State Butterfly

- is the mourning cloak
- was designated as the state butterfly in 2001
- can live as long as 10 months as adults

Key
☆ State Capital
● City

Interesting Fact

Nebraska was called The Great American Desert.

Did you know?

Nebraska became the 37th state on March 1, 1867.

Fun Fact

Beautiful Nebraska is the official state song.

Niobrara River

Scottsbluff

Nebraska

Norfolk

North Platte River

Columbus

Fremont

North Platte

Grand Island

Omaha

South Platte River

Platte River

Lincoln

McCook

Hastings

Republican River

Beatrice

Official State Flag

• was adopted in 1925
• has the state seal in the colors gold and silver with the state motto Equality Before the Law
• has the date of Nebraska's admission to the union which was March 1, 1867

Official State Soft Drink

- is Kool-Aid
- was designated as the state soft drink in 1998
- is an artificially fruit-flavored powder created in 1927

Official State Fossil

- is the mammoth
- was designated as the state fossil in 1967
- most Nebraska counties has found mammoth fossils

Nebraska Quarter

- features Chimney Rock
- also features a wagon
- has the year 1867 which was when Nebraska became a state

Official State Flower

- is the goldenrod
- was designated as the state flower in 1895
- original legislation referred to it as Solidago serotina

Official State Tree

- is the cottonwood
- was designated as the state tree in 1972
- is often associated with pioneer Nebraska

Nevada

State motto: All for Our Country

Did you know?

Nevada became the 36th state on October 31, 1864.

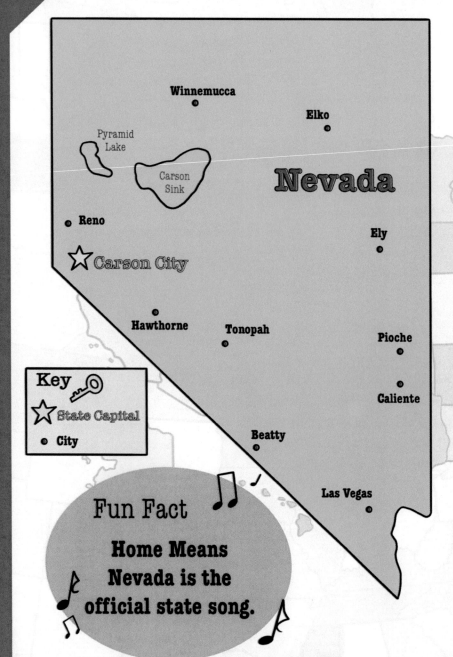

Winnemucca

Elko

Pyramid Lake

Carson Sink

Nevada

Reno

Ely

⭐ Carson City

Hawthorne

Tonopah

Pioche

Caliente

Key 🔑
⭐ State Capital
• City

Beatty

Las Vegas

Fun Fact

Home Means Nevada is the official state song.

Official State Flag

- was adopted in 1929
- has a ribbon that reads BATTLE BORN
- has a green sagebrush with yellow flowers

Official State Animal

- is the desert bighorn sheep
- was designated as the state animal in 1973
- can weigh as much as 200 pounds

Nevada Quarter

- features wild mustangs
- also features the state flower sagebrush
- has the state nickname The Silver State

Official State Flower

- is the sagebrush
- was designated as the state flower in 1917
- also called big sagebrush, common sagebrush, black sagebrush, or blue sagebrush

Official State Grass

- is the Indian ricegrass
- was designated as the state grass in 1977
- was a food source for Native Americans

Official State Seal

- the silver miner represents mineral resources
- the telegraph poles and the train steaming represents communication and transportation
- has the state motto All for Our Country

Key

⭐ State Capital

• City

State motto: Live Free or Die

Interesting Fact

The first free public library in the United States was established in 1833.

Fun Fact

Old New Hampshire is the official state song.

Did you know?

New Hampshire became the 9th state on June 21, 1788.

Official State Flag

- was adopted in 1909
- has the ship Raleigh
- has the words SEAL OF THE STATE OF NEW HAMPSHIRE 1776

New Hampshire

Berlin

Conway

Lake Winnepesaukee

Hanover

Lebanon

Franklin

Merrimack River

Dover

Concord ⭐

Manchester

Portsmouth

Keene

Nashua

Official State Fruit

- is pumpkin
- was designated as the state fruit in 2006
- has the world record for the highest number of lit jack-o'-lanterns

New Hampshire Quarter

- features the Old Man of the Mountain
- also features the state motto Live Free or Die
- has the year 1788 which was when New Hampshire became a state

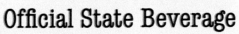

Official State Beverage

- is apple cider
- was designated as the state beverage in 2010
- New Hampshire has around 150 apple growers

Official State Bird

- is the purple finch
- was designated as the state bird in 1957
- also known as Carpodacus purpureus

Official State Flower

- is the purple lilac
- was designated as the state flower in 1919
- there are over 1,000 varieties of lilacs

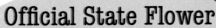

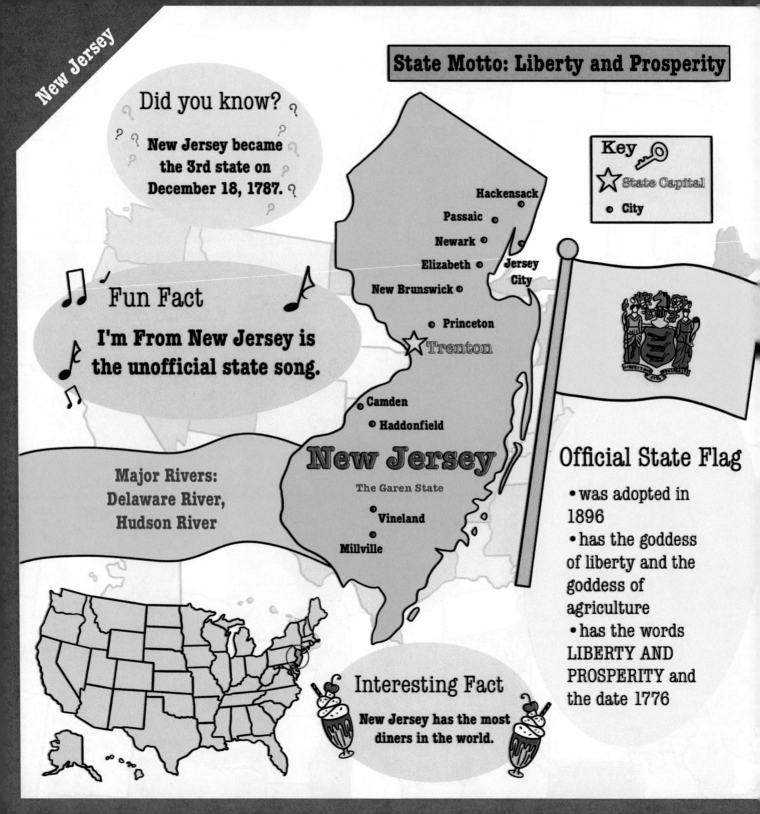

Official State Flower

- is violet
- was adopted as the state flower in 1913
- are usually see in meadows, lawns, and fields

Official State Memorial Tree

- is the dogwood
- was designated as the state memorial tree in 1951
- the wood was valued for making arrows and tool handles

Official State Tree

- is the northern red oak
- was designated as the state tree in 1950
- has been used for fence posts, flooring, and firewood

New Jersey Quarter

- features George Washington crossing the Delaware River
- also features James Monroe holding the flag
- has the year 1787 which was when New Jersey became a state

NEW JERSEY 1787

CROSSROADS OF THE REVOLUTION

1999

E PLURIBUS UNUM

Key
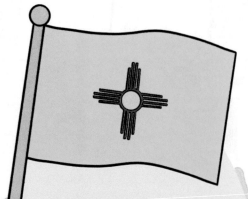

⭐ State Capital

• City

Did you know?

New Mexico became the 47th state on January 6, 1912.

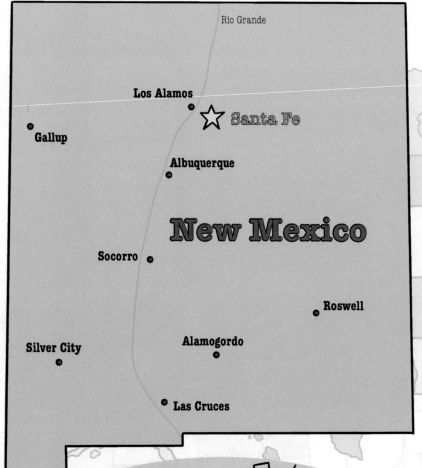

Rio Grande

Los Alamos

⭐ Santa Fe

Gallup

Albuquerque

New Mexico

Socorro

Roswell

Alamogordo

Silver City

Las Cruces

Official State Flag

• was picked from a flag competition in 1920
• they used the colors red and yellow because they were the colors of the flag of the Spanish conquistadors
• has a design based off an ancient Sun symbol called a Zia

Fun Fact

O, Fair New Mexico is the official state song.

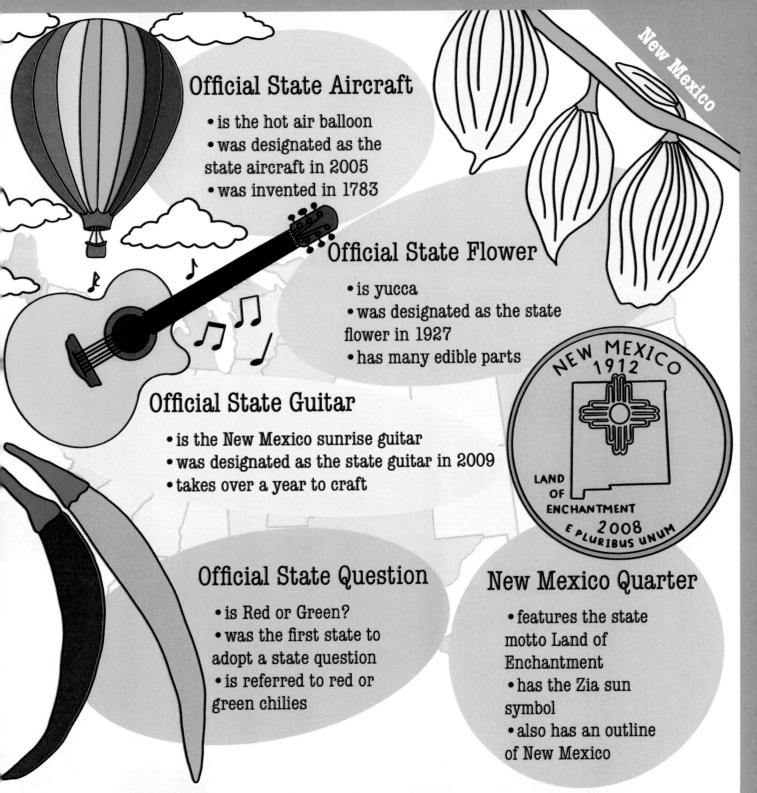

Official State Aircraft

- is the hot air balloon
- was designated as the state aircraft in 2005
- was invented in 1783

Official State Flower

- is yucca
- was designated as the state flower in 1927
- has many edible parts

Official State Guitar

- is the New Mexico sunrise guitar
- was designated as the state guitar in 2009
- takes over a year to craft

NEW MEXICO
1912
LAND
OF
ENCHANTMENT
2008
E PLURIBUS UNUM

Official State Question

- is Red or Green?
- was the first state to adopt a state question
- is referred to red or green chilies

New Mexico Quarter

- features the state motto Land of Enchantment
- has the Zia sun symbol
- also has an outline of New Mexico

**State Motto: Excelsior
(Ever Upwards)**

Interesting Fact

In 1901, New York became the first state to require license plates on cars.

Key
⭐ State Capital
● City

New York

● Buffalo ● Rochester
● Syracuse
⭐ Albany

Fun Fact
I Love New York is the official state song.

Did you know?
New York became the 11th state on July 26, 1788.

Major Rivers: Hudson River, Mohawk River, Genesee River

● New York City
Long Island

Official State Flag
- was adopted in 1901
- features 2 women named Liberty and Justice (Liberty symbolizes freedom and Justice symbolizes justice before the law)
- has the word EXCELSIOR on the white ribbon

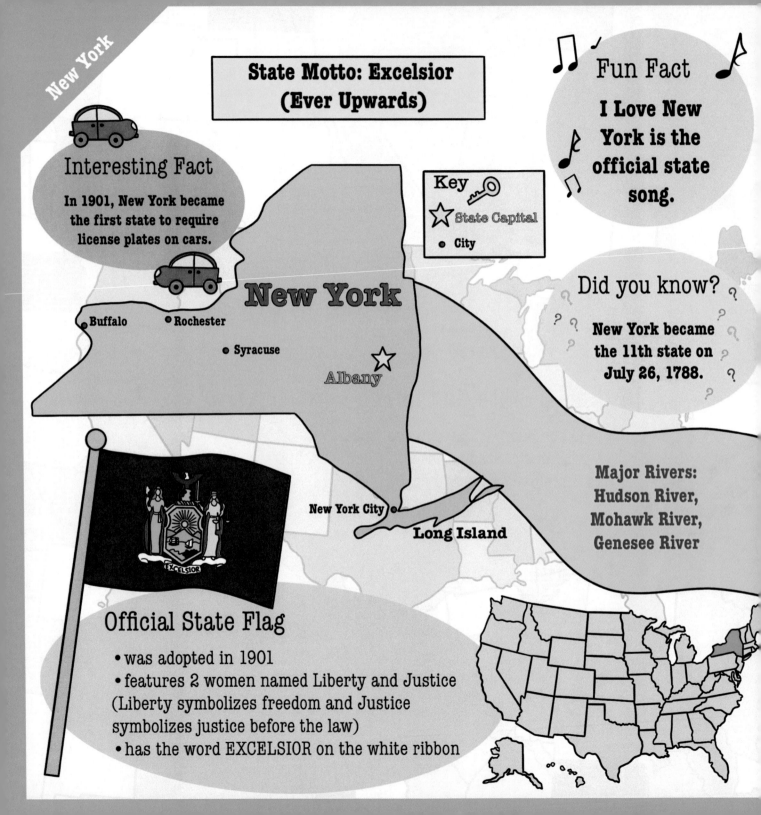

Official State Flower

- is rose
- was designated as the state flower in 1955
- has been around for 35 million years

Official State Snack

- is yogurt
- was designated as the state snack in 2014
- can also be spelled yoghurt, yogourt, or yoghourt

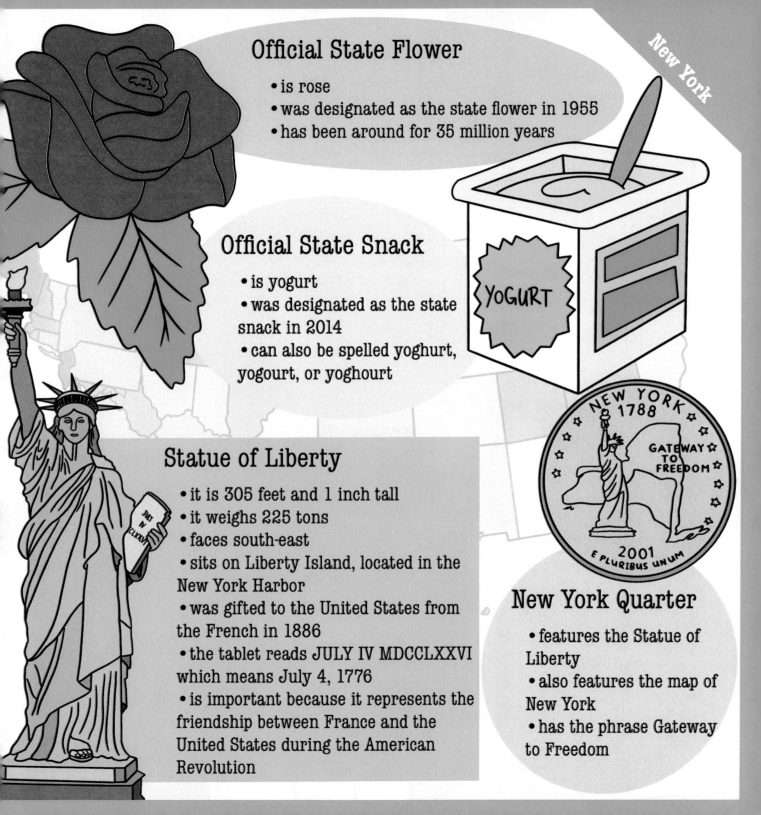

Statue of Liberty

- it is 305 feet and 1 inch tall
- it weighs 225 tons
- faces south-east
- sits on Liberty Island, located in the New York Harbor
- was gifted to the United States from the French in 1886
- the tablet reads JULY IV MDCCLXXVI which means July 4, 1776
- is important because it represents the friendship between France and the United States during the American Revolution

New York Quarter

- features the Statue of Liberty
- also features the map of New York
- has the phrase Gateway to Freedom

North Carolina

Tar Heel State

Interesting Fact

Krispy Kreme Doughnut was founded in Winston-Salem in 1937.

State Motto: Esse Quam Videri (To Be Rather Than to Seem)

Key

⭐ State Capital

• City

Winston-Salem

Durham

⭐ Raleigh

Charlotte

Official State Flag

MAY 20th 1775

N ⭐ C

APRIL 12th 1776

- was adopted in 1885
- has the date May 20th, 1775 which recalls the Mecklenburg Declaration of Independence
- also has the date April 12th, 1776 which recalls the adoption of the Halifax Resolves

Did you know?

North Carolina became the 12th state on November 21, 1789.

Fun Fact

The Old North State is the official state song.

Major Lakes: Lake Mattamuskeet, Lake Phelps, Lake Waccamaw

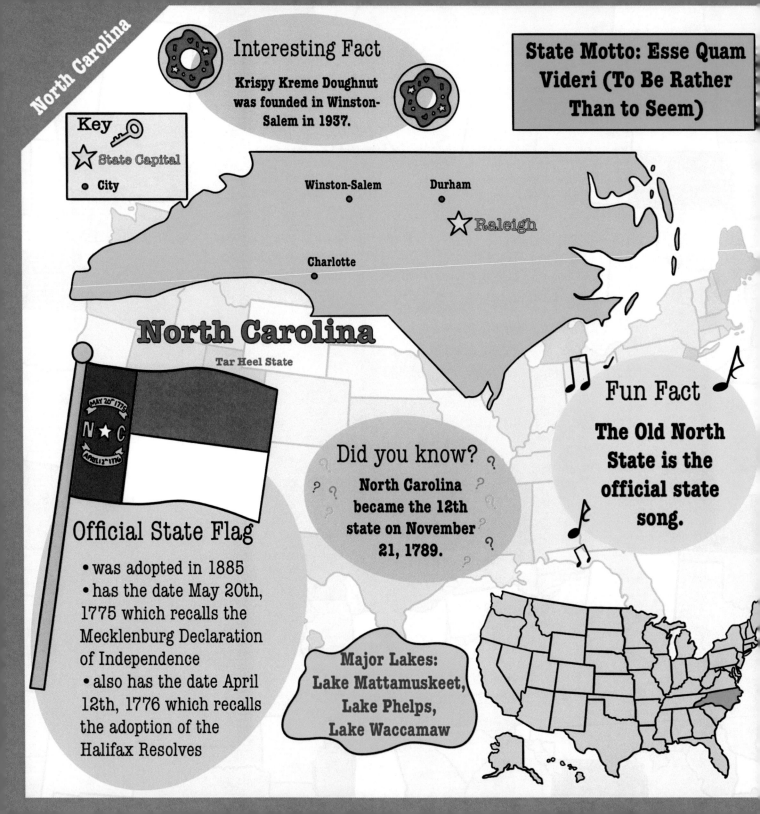

Official State Art Medium

- is clay
- was designated as the state art medium in 2013
- contributes to North Carolina's social, cultural, and economic prosperity

Official State Fossil

- is the megalodon shark teeth
- was designated as the state fossil in 2013
- the megalodon shark teeth grew over 7 inches in length

NORTH CAROLINA
1789
FIRST FLIGHT
2001
E PLURIBUS UNUM

North Carolina Quarter

- features the first flight
- has the year 1789 which was when North Carolina became a state
- was issued in 2001

Official State Precious Stone

- is emerald
- was designated as the state precious Stone in 1973
- more than 300 minerals have been found in North Carolina

Key
⭐ State Capital
• City

North Dakota

Peace Garden State

Did you know?

North Dakota became the 39th state on November 2, 1889.

Williston

Minot

Lake Sakakawea

Devil's Lake

James River

Grand Forks

Dickinson

⭐ Bismarck

Jamestown

Fargo

Missouri River

Fun Fact

North Dakota Hymn is the official state song.

Interesting Fact

North Dakota produces more sunflowers than any other state.

Official State Flag

- was adopted in 1911
- has the USA state motto E PLURIBUS UNUM which means Out of Many, One
- has an eagle holding an olive branch and 7 arrows

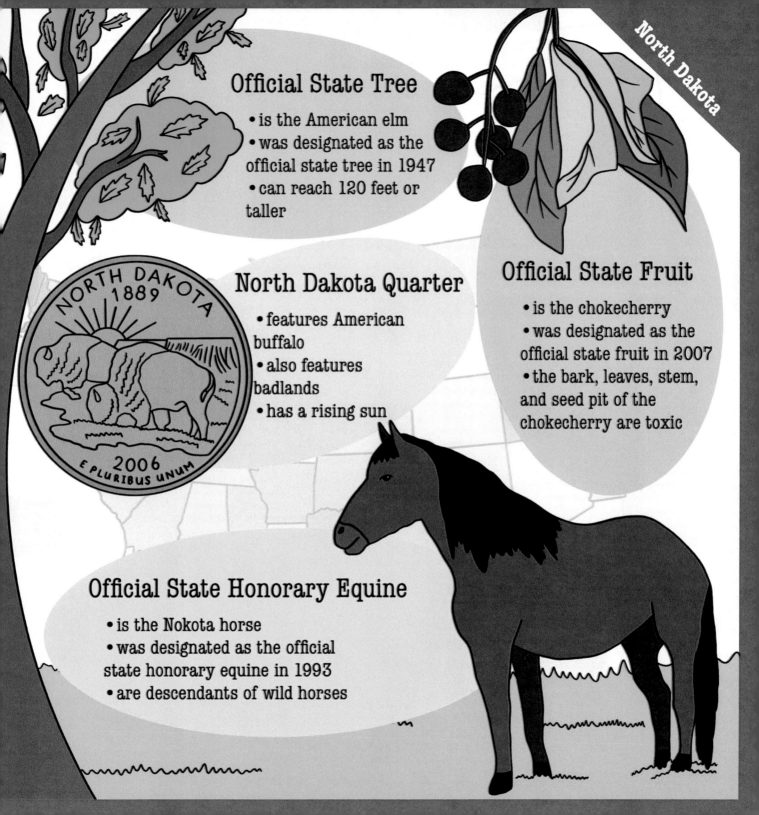

Official State Tree

- is the American elm
- was designated as the official state tree in 1947
- can reach 120 feet or taller

North Dakota Quarter

- features American buffalo
- also features badlands
- has a rising sun

Official State Fruit

- is the chokecherry
- was designated as the official state fruit in 2007
- the bark, leaves, stem, and seed pit of the chokecherry are toxic

Official State Honorary Equine

- is the Nokota horse
- was designated as the official state honorary equine in 1993
- are descendants of wild horses

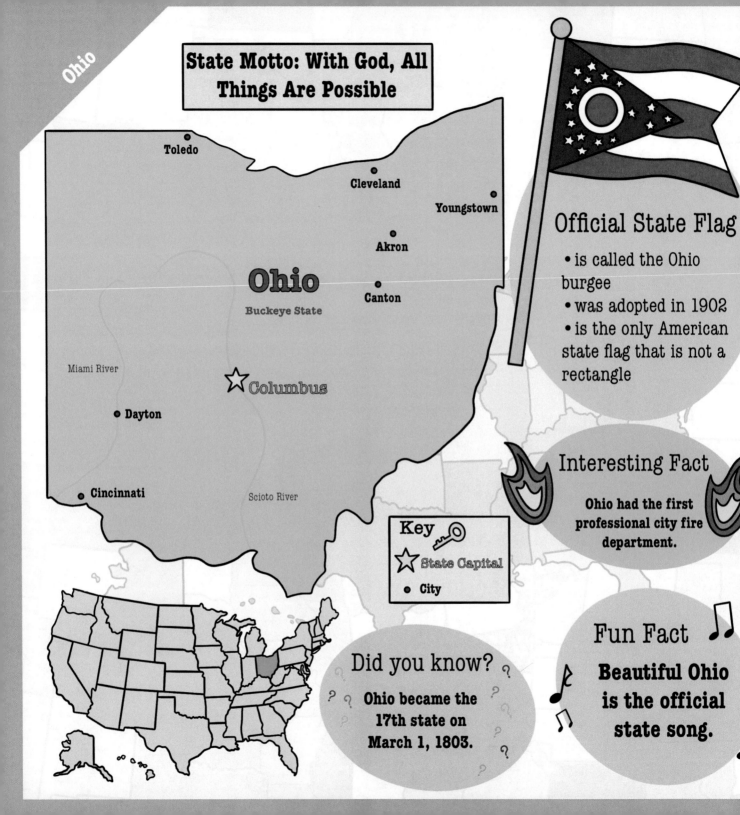

Ohio

State Motto: With God, All Things Are Possible

Toledo

Cleveland

Youngstown

Akron

Ohio

Canton

Buckeye State

Miami River

☆ Columbus

● Dayton

● Cincinnati

Scioto River

Key

☆ State Capital
● City

Official State Flag

• is called the Ohio burgee
• was adopted in 1902
• is the only American state flag that is not a rectangle

Interesting Fact

Ohio had the first professional city fire department.

Did you know?

Ohio became the 17th state on March 1, 1803.

Fun Fact

Beautiful Ohio is the official state song.

Official State Flower

- is the red carnation
- was designated as the official state flower in 1904
- the scientific name is dianthus caryophyllus

OHIO
1803

BIRTHPLACE
OF AVIATION
PIONEERS

DW

2002

E PLURIBUS UNUM

Ohio

Ohio Quarter

- features an astronaut
- also features the outline of the state
- has the caption Birthplace of Aviation Pioneers

TOMATO JUICE

Official State Beverage

- is tomato juice
- was designated as the official state beverage in 1965
- one of the top tomato producing states is Ohio

Official State Wildflower

- is the white trillium
- was designated as the official state wildflower in 1986
- is found in 88 counties of Ohio

State Motto: Labor omnia vincit
(Labor Conquers All Things)

Enid

Tulsa

Oklahoma

Muskogee

Elk City

☆ Oklahoma City

Norman

Arkansas River

Lawton

Canadian River

Official State Flag

• was adopted in 1925
• has a gray peace pipe also called a calumet
• also has an olive branch with eagle feathers

Did you know?

Oklahoma became the 46th state on November 16, 1907.

Major Lakes:
Eufaula Lake,
Lake Hudson,
Lake Texoma,

Interesting Fact

Oklahoma was the world's first place to install a parking meter.

Fun Fact

Oklahoma is the official state song.

Official State Vegetable

- is watermelon
- was designated as the state vegetable in 2007
- scientific name is citrullus lanatus

Official State Flying Mammal

- is the Mexican free-tailed bat
- was designated as the state flying mammal in 2006
- are nocturnal animals and hunt insects using echolocation

Official State Wildflower

- is the Indian blanket
- was designated as the state wildlower in 1986
- also called firewheel

Oklahoma Quarter

- features the state bird called scissor-tailed flycatcher
- also features the state wildflower called Indian blankets
- has the year 1907 which was when Oklahoma became a state

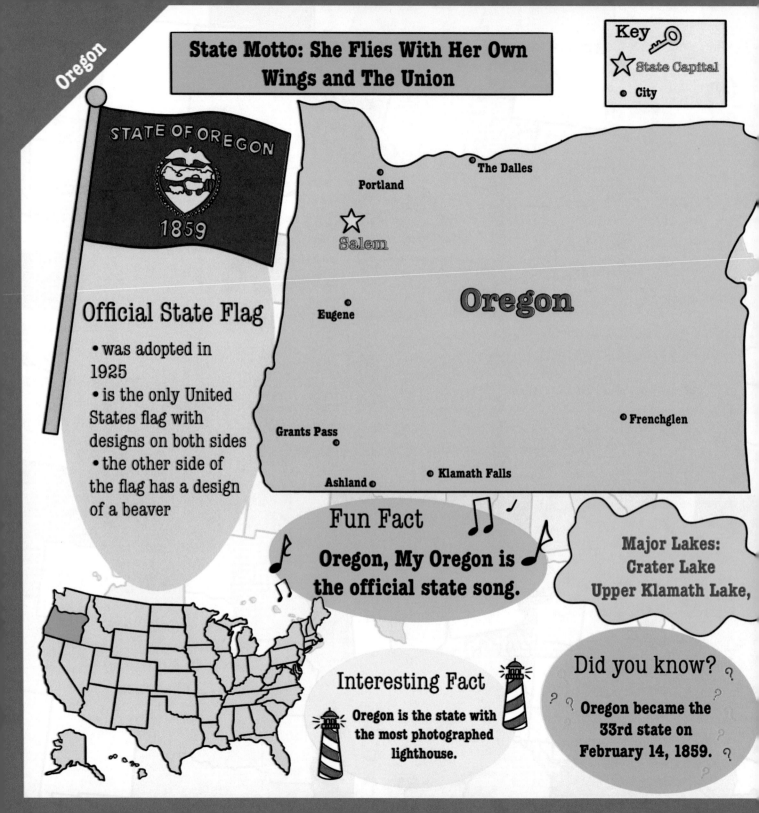

Oregon

State Motto: She Flies With Her Own Wings and The Union

Key
☆ State Capital
● City

STATE OF OREGON
1859

The Dalles
Portland
☆ Salem

Oregon

Eugene

Frenchglen

Grants Pass

Ashland ● ● Klamath Falls

Official State Flag

- was adopted in 1925
- is the only United States flag with designs on both sides
- the other side of the flag has a design of a beaver

Fun Fact
Oregon, My Oregon is the official state song.

Major Lakes:
**Crater Lake
Upper Klamath Lake,**

Interesting Fact
Oregon is the state with the most photographed lighthouse.

Did you know?
Oregon became the 33rd state on February 14, 1859.

Official State Fruit

- is the pear
- was designated as the state fruit in 2005
- over 20 species of pears

Oregon Quarter

- features Crater Lake National Park
- has the year 1859 which was when Oregon became a state
- was released in 2005

OREGON
1859

CRATER LAKE

2005
E PLURIBUS UNUM

Official State Flower

- is the Oregon grape
- was designated as the state flower in 1899
- also called holly-leaved barberry

Official State Crustacean

- is the dungeness crab
- was designated as the state crustacean in 2009
- is important to Oregon's economy

State Motto: Virtue, Liberty, and Independence

Pennsylvania

Allegheny River

Ohio River • **Pittsburgh**

Monongahela River

Harrisburg
☆

Philadelphia

Susquehanna River

Interesting Fact

In 1784, the first daily newspaper was published in Pennsylvania.

NEWS

NEWS

Did you know?

Pennsylvania became the 2nd state on December 12, 1787.

Key
🔑
☆ State Capital
• City

Fun Fact

Pennsylvania is the official state song.

Major Lake: Lake Erie

Official State Flag

- was adopted in 1907
- features 2 horses, a ship, a stalk of a corn, an olive branch, wheat, and a plow
- says VIRTUE LIBERTY INDEPENDENCE

Official State Toy

- is the slinky
- was designated as the state toy in 2001
- was invented in 1943

PENNSYLVANIA 1787

VIRTUE LIBERTY INDEPENDENCE

1999

Pennsylvania Quarter

- features an outline of the state Pennsylvania
- has a statue representing commonwealth
- has the state motto VIRTUE LIBERTY INDEPENDENCE

Official State Tree

- is the eastern hemlock
- was designated as the state tree in 1931
- was used by early settlers to make log cabins

Official State Plant

- is the penngift crownvetch
- was designated as the state plant in 1982
- was first discovered in 1935

State motto: Hope

Rhode Island

Providence

- Woonsocket
- Cranston
- West Warwick
- East Greenwich
- W. Kingston
- Westerly

Prudence Island

Conanicut Island

Aquidneck Island

Block Island

Key
- ⭐ State Capital
- • City

Official State Flag

- was adopted in 1897
- has a yellow anchor with 13 stars
- also has a blue ribbon with the word HOPE

Fun Fact 🎵

Rhode Island, It's for Me is the official state song.

Interesting Fact

Rhode Island is known for making fine jewelry.

Did you know?

Rhode Island became the 13th state on May 29, 1790.

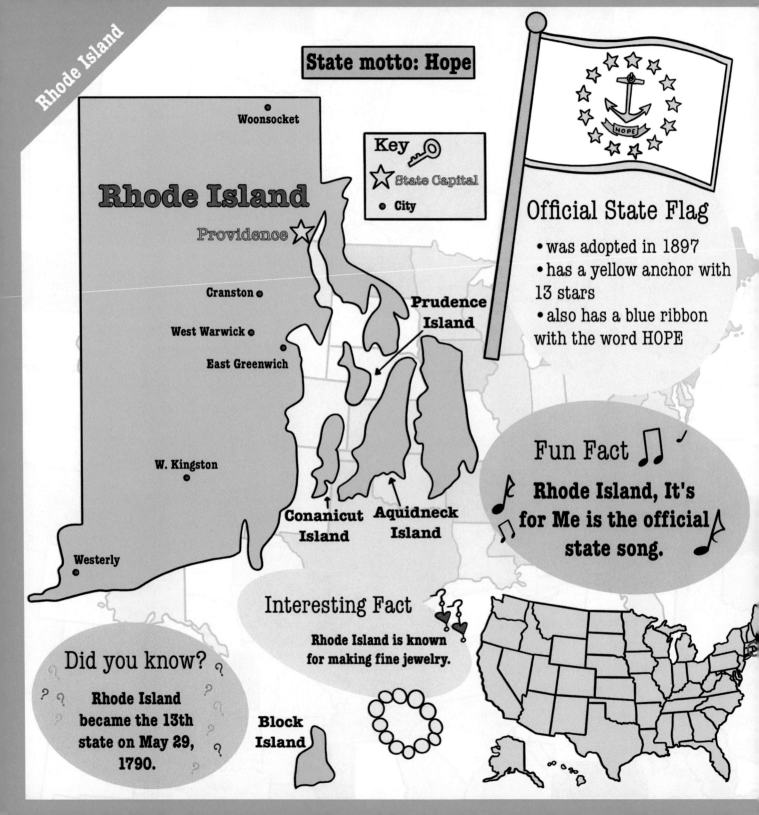

Official State Bird

- is the red chicken
- was designated the state bird in 1954
- popular for their egg laying abilities

Official State Fruit

- is the greening apple
- was designated the state fruit in 1991
- was developed around 1796

Rhode Island Quarter

- has the state nickname The Ocean State
- features Pell Bridge
- also features America's Cup yacht Reliance

Official State Flower

- is violet
- was designated the state flower in 1968
- has around 500 species

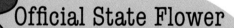

Official State Drink

- is coffee milk
- was designated the state drink in 1993
- is made with coffee syrup

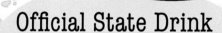

South Carolina

**State Motto: Dum Spiro Spero
(While I breathe, I hope)**

Spartanburg

Greenville

South Carolina

Florence

☆
Columbia

Sumter

Fun Fact
Carolina is the official state song.

Interesting Fact
South Carolina has the world's largest Gingko farm.

Key
☆ State Capital
• City

Charleston

**Major Rivers:
Edisto River,
Santee River,
Savannah River**

**Major Lakes:
Lake Marion,
Lake Moultrie**

Official State Flag
• was adopted in 1861
• features a white crescent
• also features white palmetto tree

Did you know?
South Carolina became the 8th state on May 23, 1788.

Official State Flower

- is the yellow jessamine
- was designated the state flower in 1924
- all parts of this flower is poisonous

Official State Spider

- is the Carolina wolf spider
- was designated the state spider in 2000
- is the largest North American wolf spider

Official State Beverage

- is the South Carolina grown tea
- was designated the state beverage in 1995
- was the first place in the USA where tea was grown

South Carolina Quarter

- features the state bird Carolina wren
- also features the state tree sabal palmetto
- has the nickname The Palmetto State

Official State Tree

- is the sabal palmetto
- was designated the state tree in 1939
- also called cabbage palm

SOUTH CAROLINA 1788
THE PALMETTO STATE
2000
E PLURIBUS UNUM

State Motto: Under God the people rule

South Dakota

Mobridge

Aberdeen

James River

Watertown

Belle Fourche

Spearfish

Cheyenne River

☆ Pierre

Huron

Rapid City

Missouri River

Mitchell

Sioux Falls

Fun Fact

Hail, South Dakota is the official state song.

Key
☆ State Capital
● City

Major Lakes:
**Lake Francis Case,
Lake Oahe,
Lewis and Clark Lake**

Did you know?

South Dakota became the 40th state on November 2, 1889.

Interesting Fact

South Dakota has the largest underground gold mine in the United States.

Official State Flag

- was adopted in 1963
- says the words South Dakota and The Mount Rushmore State
- has the state seal in the center

Official State Bread

- is fry bread
- was designated as the state bread in 2005
- also known as squaw bread

Official State Dessert

- is kuchen
- was designated as the state dessert in 2000
- kuchen is the German word for cake

Official State Tree

- is the Black Hills white spruce
- was designated as the state tree in 1947
- can range from 30 to 60 feet in height

South Dakota Quarter

- features the state bird called ring-necked pheasant
- also features Mount Rushmore
- has the year 1889 which was when South Dakota became a state

SOUTH DAKOTA 1889 · 2006 · E PLURIBUS UNUM

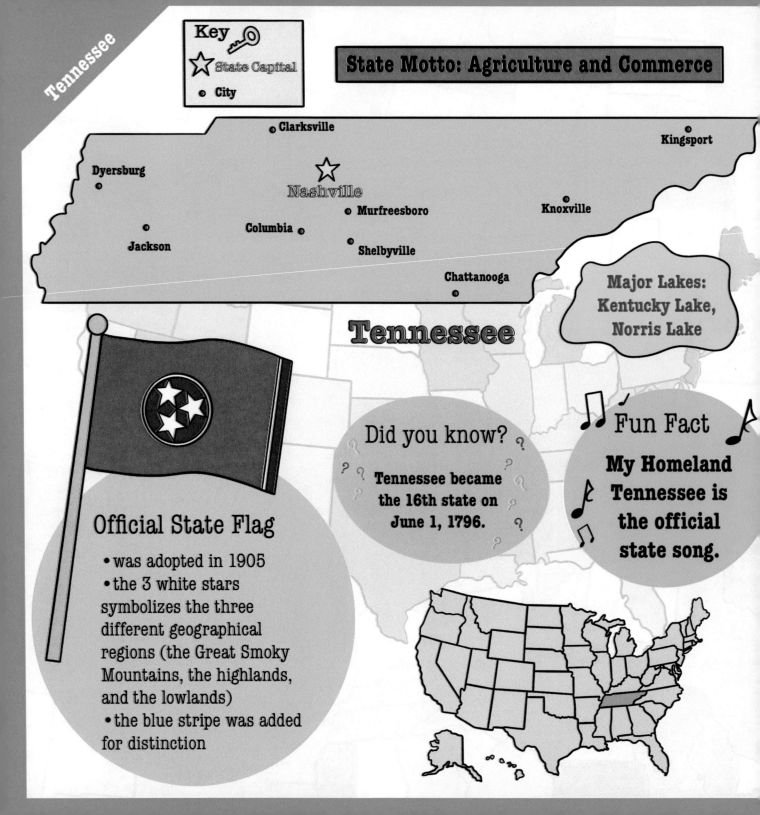

Tennessee

Key
☆ State Capital
• City

Clarksville

Kingsport

Dyersburg

☆ Nashville

Murfreesboro

Knoxville

Columbia

Jackson

Shelbyville

Chattanooga

Tennessee

Major Lakes:
Kentucky Lake,
Norris Lake

Did you know?

Tennessee became the 16th state on June 1, 1796.

Fun Fact

My Homeland Tennessee is the official state song.

Official State Flag

• was adopted in 1905
• the 3 white stars symbolizes the three different geographical regions (the Great Smoky Mountains, the highlands, and the lowlands)
• the blue stripe was added for distinction

Official State Pets

- are rescued dogs and cats
- was designated as the state pet in 2014
- the US currently has around 6 million pets in animal shelters

Tennessee Quarter

- honors the state's musical heritage
- features a fiddle, trumpet, guitar, and sheet music
- has the year 1796 which was when Tennessee became a state

Official State Seal

- features the plow, wheat ,and cotton stalk which are symbols of Tennessee's agriculture
- also features a riverboat
- has the Roman numeral XVI to show that Tennessee was the 16th state

Official State Wildflower

- is the Tennessee purple coneflower
- was designated as one of the state wildflowers in 2012
- are only found in the limestone and cedar glades of Middle Tennessee

Texas

The Lone Star State

State motto: Friendship

Did you know?

Texas became the 28th state on December 29, 1845.

Key

★ State Capital

• City

Amarillo

Lubbock

Abilene

Dallas

Fort Worth

El Paso

Waco

Austin ★

Houston

Laredo

Brownsville

Major Rivers:
Rio Grande,
Red River,
Brazos River

Fun Fact

Texas, Our Texas is the official state song.

Official State Flag

- was adopted in 1845
- is called the Lone Star Flag
- the colors blue represents loyalty, red represents bravery, and white represents purity

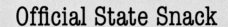

Official State Snack

- is chips and salsa
- was designated as the state snack in 2003
- salsa is the Spanish word for sauce

Official State Fruit

- is the Texas red grapefruit
- was designated as the state fruit in 1993
- Texans has been growing grapefruit for over 100 years

Texas Quarter

- features an outline of the state Texas
- also features the famous Lone Star
- has the states nickname The Lone Star

Official State Footwear

- is the cowboy boot
- was designated as the state footwear in 2007
- originated in the 1800s

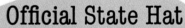

Official State Hat

- is the cowboy hat
- was designated as the state hat in 2015
- was invented in 1865

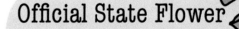

Official State Flower

- is the bluebonnet
- was designated as the state flower in 1901
- was named for their blue color

Key

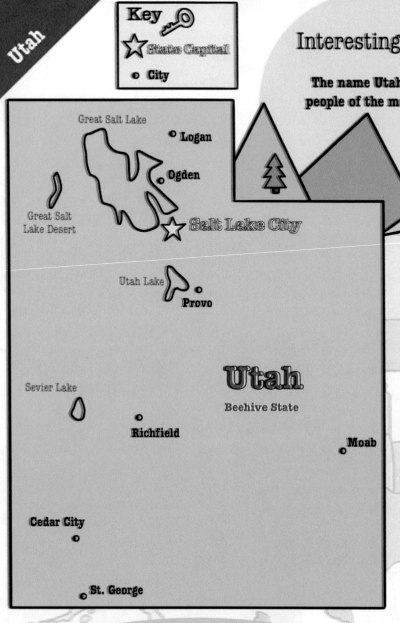

☆ State Capital

• City

Interesting Fact

The name Utah means people of the mountains

Great Salt Lake

• Logan

○ Ogden

Great Salt Lake Desert

☆ Salt Lake City

Utah Lake

• Provo

Utah

Beehive State

Sevier Lake

○ Richfield

• Moab

Cedar City ○

• St. George

Official State Flag

• was adopted in 1913
• features the state seal in the center
• has the word INDUSTRY

Fun Fact

Utah, We Love Thee is the official state song.

Official State Symbol

- is the Beehive cluster
- was designated as the state symbol in 1996
- is a large, bright, and open cluster of stars

Official State Fruit

- is cherry
- was designated as the state fruit in 1997
- around 2 billion cherries are harvested every year

Official State Flower

- is the sego lily
- was designated as the state flower in 1911
- also called mariposa lily

Official State Bird

- is the California Gull
- was designated as the state bird in 1955
- agriculturalists consider this bird to be very beneficial

Utah Quarter

- features a golden spike
- also features two locomotives
- says the words CROSSROADS OF THE WEST

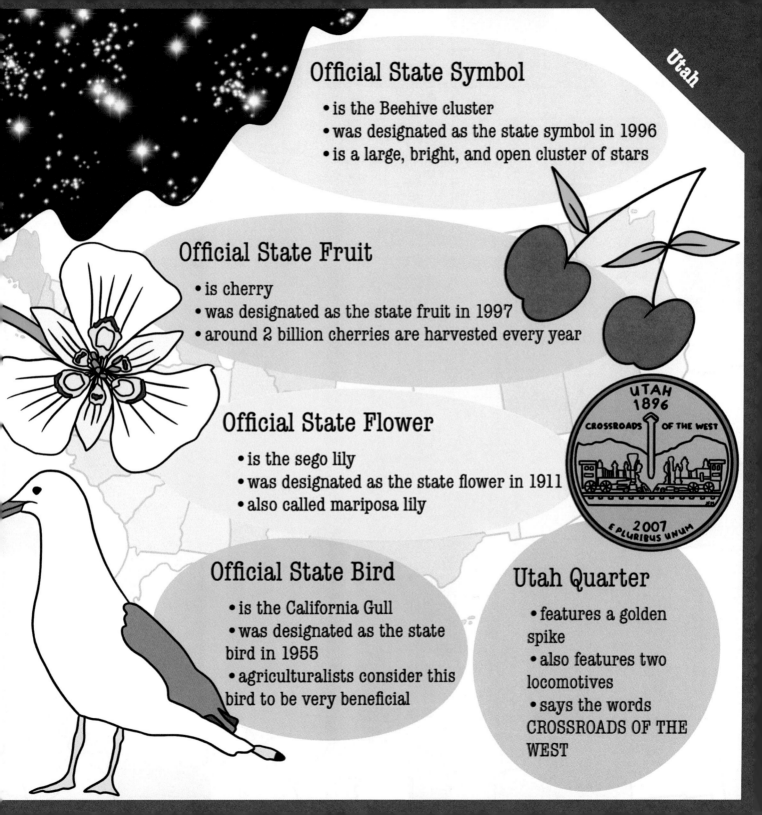

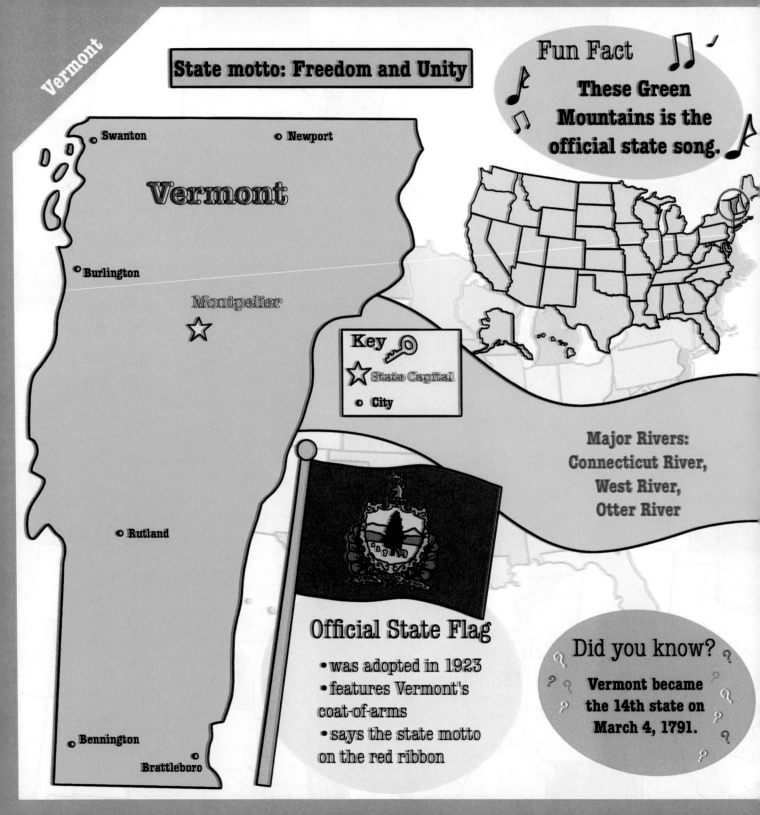

Vermont

State motto: Freedom and Unity

Vermont

- Swanton
- Newport

- Burlington

Montpelier
⭐

Key 🔑
⭐ State Capital
○ City

- Rutland

- Bennington
- Brattleboro

Fun Fact
These Green Mountains is the official state song.

Major Rivers:
Connecticut River,
West River,
Otter River

Official State Flag
- was adopted in 1923
- features Vermont's coat-of-arms
- says the state motto on the red ribbon

Did you know?
Vermont became the 14th state on March 4, 1791.

Official State Heritage Breed of Livestock

- is the Randall lineback breed of cattle
- was designated as the state heritage breed of livestock in 2006
- bos taurus is the scientific name

Official State Pie

- is the apple pie
- was designated as the state pie in 1999
- the first recorded recipe was written in 1381

Vermont Quarter

- features Camel's Hump Mountain
- also features sugar maple trees with sap buckets
- says a the state motto

Official State Flavor

- is maple
- was designated as the state flavor in 1993
- Vermont produces over 500,000 gallons of maple syrup a year

Official State Flower

- is the red clover
- was designated as the state flower in 1894
- trifolium pratense is the scientific name

State Motto: Sic Semper Tyrannis (Thus Always to Tyrants)

Fun Fact

Carry Me Back to Old Virginia is the official state song.

Did you know?

Virginia became the 10th state on June 25, 1788.

Arlington

Virginia

Richmond

Lynchburg

Roanoke

Danville

Key

⭐ State Capital

○ City

Major Lakes: Pound Lake, Philpott Lake

Official State Flag

- was adopted in 1861
- says the words VIRGINIA and SIC SEMPER TYRANNIS which is Latin for thus always to tyrants
- features the goddess Virtue who has defeated a tyrant

Major Rivers: James River, Rappahannock River, Potomac River, Shenandoah River

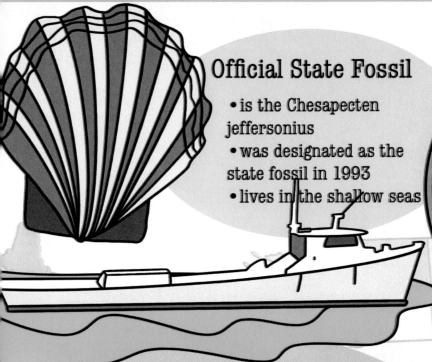

Official State Fossil

- is the Chesapecten jeffersonius
- was designated as the state fossil in 1993
- lives in the shallow seas

Official State Boat

- is the classic Chesapeake Bay Deadrise
- was designated as the state boat in 1988
- was developed around the 1880s

Official State Dog

- is the American foxhound
- was designated as the state dog in 1966
- their lifespan is 10-12 years

Virginia Quarter

- features the Jamestown colonial ships Susan Constant, Godspeed, and Discovery
- says the words Jamestown 1607-2007 and QUADRICENTENNIAL
- has the year 1788 which was when Virginia became a state

State Motto: Alki which means By and By

Washington

- Bellingham
- Everett
- Seattle
- Renton
- Tacoma
- ☆ Olympia
- Wenatchee
- Spokane
- Yakima
- Kennewick

Major Lake: Lake Washington

Key
- ☆ State Capital
- • City

Fun Fact

Washington, My Home is the official state song.

Did you know?

Washington became the 42nd state on November 11, 1889.

Official State Flag

- was adopted in 1923
- features George Washington
- says the words THE SEAL OF THE STATE OF WASHINGTON

THE SEAL OF THE STATE OF WASHINGTON 1889

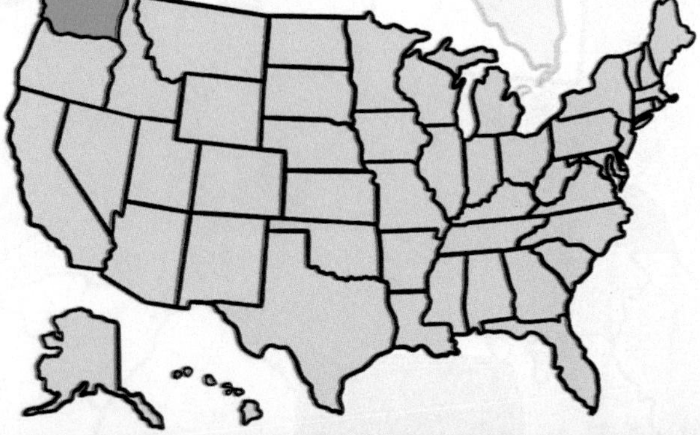

Official State Tree

- is the western hemlock
- was designated as the state tree in 1947
- grows from 50-70 meters tall

Official State Insect

- is the green darner dragonfly
- was designated as the state insect in 1997
- is one of the fastest-flying dragonflies

Washington Quarter

- features a leaping salmon, Mount Rainier, and the western hemlocks
- also features the state nickname The Evergreen State
- has the year 1889 which was when Washington became a state

Official State Flower

- is the coast rhododendron
- was designated as the state flower in 1959
- also called Pacific rhododendron or big leaf rhododendron

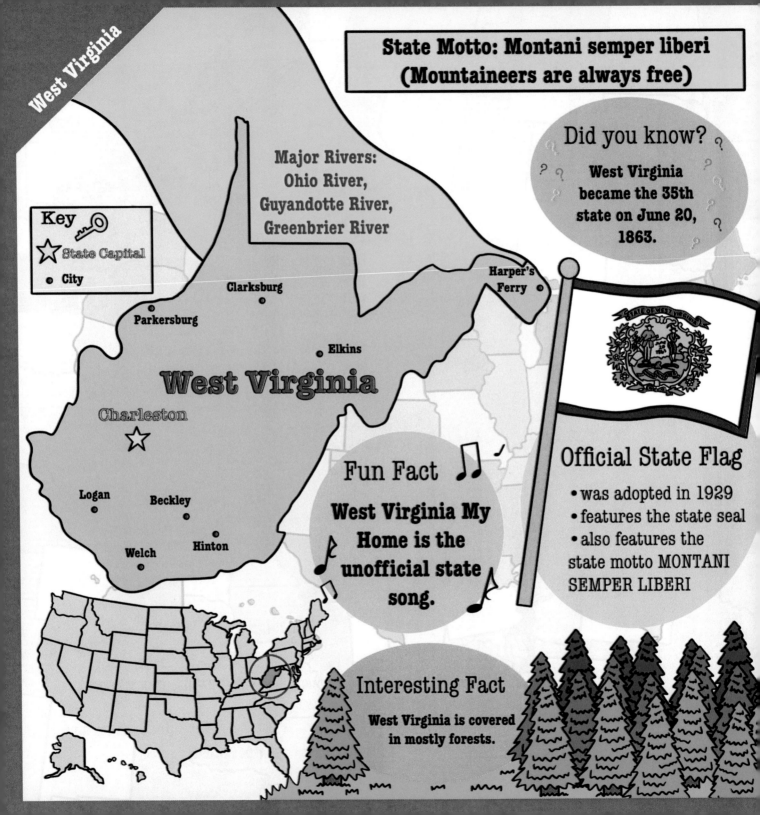

West Virginia

**State Motto: Montani semper liberi
(Mountaineers are always free)**

Major Rivers:
Ohio River,
Guyandotte River,
Greenbrier River

Did you know?
West Virginia
became the 35th
state on June 20,
1863.

Key
☆ State Capital
• City

Harper's
Ferry

Clarksburg

Parkersburg

Elkins

West Virginia

Charleston

Logan Beckley

Welch Hinton

Fun Fact 🎵
**West Virginia My
Home is the
unofficial state
song.**

Official State Flag
• was adopted in 1929
• features the state seal
• also features the
state motto MONTANI
SEMPER LIBERI

Interesting Fact
West Virginia is covered
in mostly forests.

Official State Flower

- is the rhododendron
- was designated as the state flower in 1903
- is a flowering shrub

West Virginia Quarter

- features the New River Gorge bridge
- has the year 1863 which was when West Virginia became a state
- was released in 2005

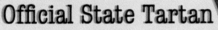

Official State Professional Theater

- is the Greenbrier Valley Theatre
- was designated as the state professional theatre in 2006
- also has shows performed by children

Official State Tartan

- is defined as a cloth and is usually made of wool
- was designated as the state tartan in 2008
- the colors were chosen to represent the mountain state's culture, history, and beauty

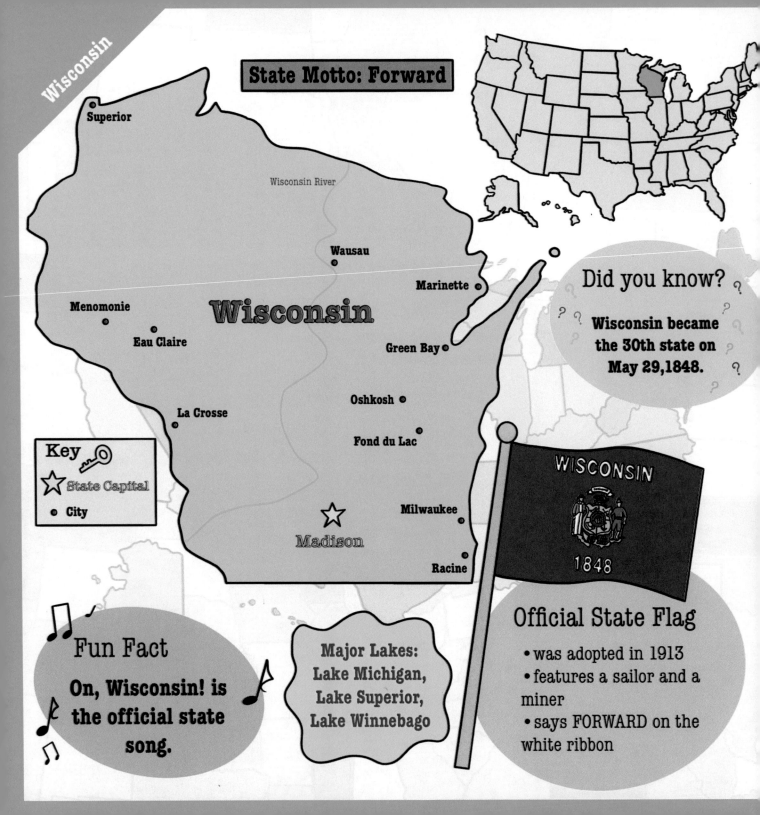

Wisconsin

State Motto: Forward

Superior

Wisconsin River

Wausau

Marinette

Menomonie

Wisconsin

Eau Claire

Green Bay

Oshkosh

La Crosse

Fond du Lac

Key

State Capital

City

Milwaukee

Madison

Racine

Did you know?

Wisconsin became the 30th state on May 29, 1848.

WISCONSIN

1848

Fun Fact

On, Wisconsin! is the official state song.

Major Lakes:
Lake Michigan,
Lake Superior,
Lake Winnebago

Official State Flag

• was adopted in 1913
• features a sailor and a miner
• says FORWARD on the white ribbon

Official State Animal

- is the badger
- was designated as the state animal in 1957
- is a ferocious fighter

Official State Symbol of Peace

- is the mourning dove
- was designated as the state symbol of peace in 1971
- was once known as the Carolina pigeon and Carolina turtledove

Official State Fruit

- is cranberry
- was designated as the state fruit in 2003
- was first named crane berry

WISCONSIN 1848
FORWARD
2004
E PLURIBUS UNUM

Wisconsin Quarter

- features the state motto FORWARD
- also features a dairy cow, a round of cheese, and an ear of corn
- has the year 1848 which was when Wisconsin became a state

Wyoming

State Motto: Equal Rights

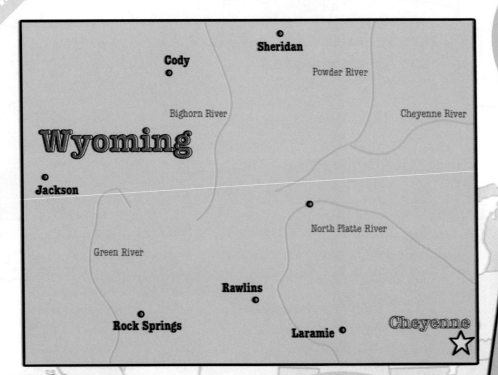

Wyoming

- Sheridan
- Cody
- Jackson
- Rawlins
- Rock Springs
- Laramie
- Cheyenne ☆

Powder River
Bighorn River
Cheyenne River
North Platte River
Green River

Fun Fact

Wyoming is the official state song.

Key 🔑
☆ State Capital
● City

Major Lake:
Bighorn Lake

Did you know?

Wyoming became the 44th state on July 10, 1890

Interesting Fact

Wyoming is the home of first official National Park.

Official State Flag

- was adopted in 1917
- features a white bison
- also features the state seal in the center which says GREAT SEAL OF THE STATE OF WYOMING

Official State Butterfly

- is the Sheridan's Green Hairstreak Butterfly
- was designated as the state butterfly in 2009
- is a symbol spring is comin in Wyoming

Official State Coin

- is the Sacajawea golden dollar
- was designated as the state coin in 2004
- has Sacagawea and her son Jean Baptiste

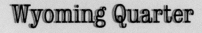

Official State Flower

- is the Indian paintbrush
- was designated as the state flower in 1917
- is also called prairie fire

Wyoming Quarter

- features the state nickname THE EQUALITY STATE
- also features an outline of a cowboy and bucking bronco
- has the year 1890 which was when Wyoming became a state

The End!

remember to:

Believe
Dream
Achieve

More Bearific® books on bearific.com

Become a member!

FOR $1, $3, or $5 A MONTH!

- get access to all digital books
- watch step by step how to draw videos (new videos are posted weekly)
- printables come from the pages in the coloring and word search book
- have exclusive voting power for new books, apps, how to draw videos and more
- receive a surprise
- watch fun cartoons based off the books
- download apps based off the books
- watch inspirational videos to stay positive
- be the first to read new books before they are available to purchase online

JOIN

Go to Bearific.com or patreon.com/bearific to join!

Katelyn Lonas

Katelyn is a 15 year old who resides in Southern California. Katelyn loves to encourage others to always believe in themselves and chase after their dreams! She started writing and illustrating her first book at age 9 and then published 41 more books. She hopes you enjoy reading this book and be ready for more books to come!

-Katelyn

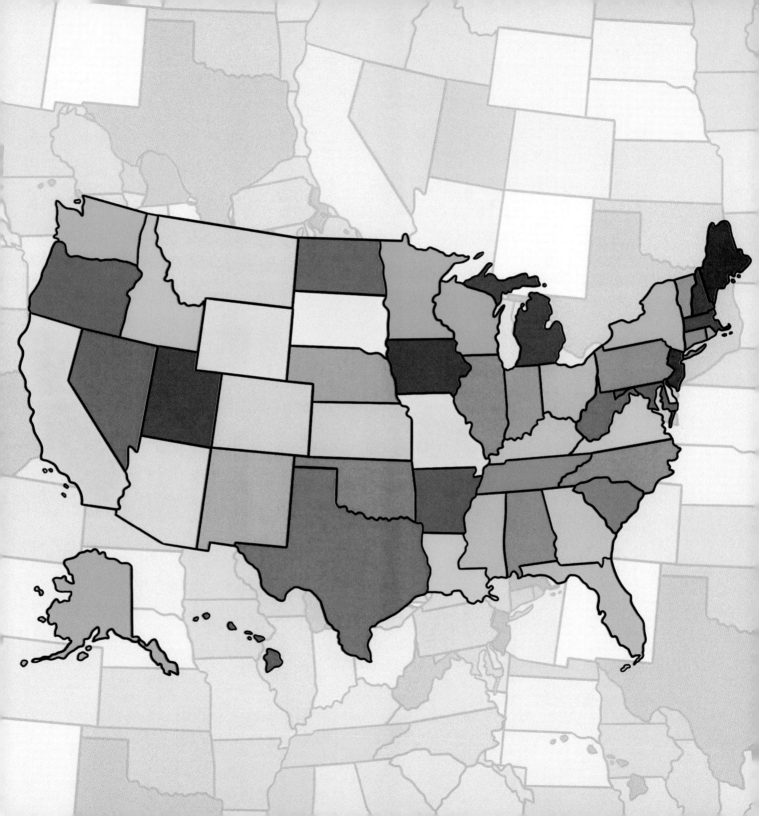

Made in the USA
Las Vegas, NV
27 September 2023

78230684R00064